# ARL ANNUAL SALARY SURVEY 2010–2011

Compiled and Edited by

MARTHA KYRILLIDOU
SHANEKA MORRIS

ASSOCIATION OF RESEARCH LIBRARIES
WASHINGTON, DC
2011

ARL Annual Salary Survey 2010–2011

The quantitative tables presented in this publication are not indicative of performance and should not be used as measures of library quality. In comparing any individual library to ARL medians or to other ARL members, one must be careful to make such comparisons within the context of differing institutional characteristics.

Custom reports based on the *Salary Survey* data are also available. Contact the ARL Statistics and Measurement Program Officer for further information.

Visit the ARL Statistics and Measurement Program online at http://www.arl.org/stats/.

Published by the
Association of Research Libraries
Washington, DC  20036
www.arl.org

ISSN 0361-5669
ISBN 1-59407-866-1
EAN 978-1-59407-866-8

∞ The paper used in this publication meets the minimum requirements of the American National Standard for Information Science and National Information Standards Organization standard—Permanence of Paper for Publications and Documents in Libraries and Archives, ANSI/NISO Z39.48-1992(R1997).

# CONTENTS

**SALARY SURVEY TRENDS 2010–2011**

Figure 1: Ethnicity/Race of Professional Staff in US ARL University Libraries, FY 2010–2011 ................ 8

Figure 2: Minority Professionals by Region in US ARL University Libraries, FY 2010–2011 .................. 9

Figure 3: Race/Ethnicity and Sex Distribution of Professional Staff in ARL University Libraries, FY 2010–2011 ........................................................................................................ 10

Figure 4: Distribution of Functional Specialist Job Sub-Codes by Type of Library .................................... 12

Figure 5: Distribution of Functional Specialist Job Sub-Codes' Average Salaries by Sex ........................ 13

Figure 6: Average Salaries and Average Years of Experience of Library Professionals in Libraries with Three, Four, and Five Step Rank Structures, FY 2010–2011 ................................................. 14

**SALARY LEVELS FOR STAFF IN ARL LIBRARIES**

Table 1: Distribution by Salary Level ........................................................................................................ 19

Table 2: Salary Trends in ARL University Libraries .................................................................................. 20

Table 3: Salary Trends in US ARL University Libraries .............................................................................. 21

Table 4: Salary Trends in Canadian ARL University Libraries ................................................................. 22

**ARL NONUNIVERSITY LIBRARIES**

Table 5: Median and Beginning Professional Salaries in ARL Nonuniversity Libraries ..................... 25

Table 6: Salary Trends in ARL Nonuniversity Libraries ............................................................................ 26

**ARL UNIVERSITY LIBRARIES**

Table 7: Filled Positions; Average, Median, and Beginning Salaries; and Average Years of Experience in ARL University Libraries, FY 2010–2011 ................................ 28

Table 8: Beginning Professional Salaries in ARL University Libraries Rank Order Table, FY 2009–2010 ........................................................................................................ 32

Table 9: Beginning Professional Salaries in ARL University Libraries Rank Order Table, FY 2010–2011 ........................................................................................................ 33

Table 10:     Median Professional Salaries in ARL University Libraries
              Rank Order Table, FY 2009–2010 ................................................................................ 34

Table 11:     Median Professional Salaries in ARL University Libraries
              Rank Order Table, FY 2010–2011 ................................................................................ 35

Table 12:     Average Professional Salaries in ARL University Libraries
              Rank Order Table, FY 2009–2010 ................................................................................ 36

Table 13:     Average Professional Salaries in ARL University Libraries
              Rank Order Table, FY 2010–2011 .................................................................................37

Table 14:     Average, Median, and Beginning Professional Salaries in ARL University Libraries
              Summary of Rankings, FYs 2007–2008 to 2010–2011 ................................................... 38

Table 15:     Distribution of Professional Staff in ARL University Libraries
              by Salary and Position, FY 2010–2011 .......................................................................... 42

Table 16:     Distribution of Professional Staff in ARL University Libraries
              by Salary, Sex, and Position, FY 2010–2011 .................................................................. 43

Table 17:     Number and Average Salaries of ARL University Librarians
              by Position and Sex, FY 2010–2011.............................................................................. 44

Table 18:     Number and Average Years of Experience of ARL University Librarians
              by Position and Sex, FY 2010–2011 .............................................................................. 45

Table 19:     Number and Average Salaries of ARL University Librarians
              by Years of Experience and Sex, FY 2010–2011 ............................................................ 46

Table 20:     Average Salaries of ARL University Librarians
              by Position and Years of Experience, FY 2010–2011 ...................................................... 47

Table 21:     Number and Average Salaries of ARL University Librarians
              by Position and Type of Institution, FY 2010–2011 ....................................................... 48

Table 22:     Years of Experience of ARL University Librarians
              by Position and Type of Institution, FY 2010–2011........................................................ 49

Table 23:     Number and Average Salaries of ARL University Librarians
              by Position and Size of Professional Staff, FY 2010–2011 .............................................. 50

Table 24:     Years of Experience of ARL University Librarians
              by Position and Size of Professional Staff, FY 2010–2011 ..............................................51

Table 25:     Average Salaries of ARL University Librarians
              by Position and Geographic Region, FY 2010–2011.......................................................52

ARL University Libraries by Geographic Region...................................................................... 53

**US ARL University Libraries**

Table 26:    Average Salaries of US ARL University Librarians
by Position and Years of Experience, FY 2010–2011 ...................................................... 56

Table 27:    Number and Average Salaries of Minority US ARL University Librarians
by Position and Sex, FY 2010–2011 ...................................................................................57

Table 28:    Number and Average Years of Experience of Minority US ARL University Librarians
by Position and Sex, FY 2010–2011 .................................................................................. 58

Table 29:    Number and Average Salaries of US ARL University Librarians
by Years of Experience and Sex, FY 2010–2011 ............................................................59

Table 30:    Number and Average Salaries of Minority US ARL University Librarians
by Years of Experience and Sex, FY 2010–2011 ............................................................ 60

**Canadian ARL University Libraries**

Table 31:    Filled Positions; Average, Median, and Beginning Professional Salaries; and Average
Years of Professional Experience in Canadian ARL University Libraries, FY 2010–2011 ........62

Table 32:    Number and Average Salaries of Canadian ARL University Librarians
by Position and Sex, FY 2010–2011 ................................................................................. 63

Table 33:    Number and Average Years of Experience of Canadian ARL University Librarians
by Position and Sex, FY 2010–2011 ................................................................................. 64

Table 34:    Number and Average Salaries of Canadian ARL University Librarians
by Years of Experience and Sex, FY 2010–2011 ........................................................... 65

**ARL University Medical Libraries**

Table 35:    Filled Positions; Average, Median, and Beginning Salaries; and Average Years of
Experience in ARL University Medical Libraries, FY 2010-2011 ............................... 68

Table 36:    Beginning Professional Salaries in ARL University Medical Libraries
Rank Order Table, FY 2010–2011 .....................................................................................70

Table 37:    Median Professional Salaries in ARL University Medical Libraries
Rank Order Table, FY 2010–2011 ..................................................................................... 71

Table 38:    Average Professional Salaries in ARL University Medical Libraries
Rank Order Table, FY 2010–2011 ..................................................................................... 72

Table 39:  Number and Average Salaries of ARL University Medical Librarians
by Position and Sex, FY 2010–2011 ................................................................................ 73

Table 40:  Number and Average Years of Experience of ARL University Medical Librarians
by Position And Sex, FY 2010–2011 ................................................................................ 74

Table 41:  Number and Average Salaries of ARL University Medical Librarians
by Years of Experience and Sex, FY 2010–2011 ........................................................... 75

## ARL University Law Libraries

Table 42:  Filled Positions; Average, Median, and Beginning Salaries; and Average Years of
Experience in ARL University Law Libraries, FY 2010–2011 ....................................... 78

Table 43:  Beginning Professional Salaries in ARL University Law Libraries
Rank Order Table, FY 2010–2011 .................................................................................. 80

Table 44:  Median Professional Salaries in ARL University Law Libraries
Rank Order Table, FY 2010–2011 .................................................................................. 81

Table 45:  Average Professional Salaries in ARL University Law Libraries
Rank Order Table, FY 2010–2011 .................................................................................. 82

Table 46:  Number and Average Salaries of ARL University Law Librarians
by Position and Sex, FY 2010–2011 ............................................................................... 83

Table 47:  Number and Average Years of Experience of ARL University Law Librarians
by Position And Sex, FY 2010–2011 ............................................................................... 84

Table 48:  Number and Average Salaries of ARL University Law Librarians
by Years of Experience and Sex, FY 2010–2011 ........................................................... 85

University Library Questionnaire and Instructions ............................................................................ 87

Nonuniversity Library Questionnaire and Instructions .................................................................... 101

Footnotes to the ARL Annual Salary Survey, 2010–2011 ................................................................ 107

ARL Member Libraries as of January 1, 2011 .................................................................................... 119

# Salary Survey Trends 2010–2011

The *ARL Annual Salary Survey 2010–2011* reports salary data for all professional staff working in Association of Research Libraries (ARL) member libraries. ARL represents the interests of libraries that serve major North American research institutions. The Association operates as a forum for the exchange of ideas and as an agent for collective action to influence forces affecting the ability of these libraries to meet the future needs of scholarship. The ARL Statistics and Assessment program, which produces the *Salary Survey*, is organized around collecting, analyzing, and distributing quantifiable information describing the characteristics of research libraries. The *ARL Annual Salary Survey* is the most comprehensive and thorough guide to current salaries in large US and Canadian academic and research libraries and is a valuable management and research tool.

Data for 10,037 professional staff members were reported this year for the 115 ARL university libraries, including their law and medical libraries (974 staff members reported by 73 medical libraries and 734 staff members reported by 77 law libraries). For the 10 nonuniversity ARL members, data were reported for 3,709 professional staff members.

The tables are organized in seven major sections. The first section includes Tables 1 through 4, which report salary figures for all professionals working in ARL member libraries, including law and medical library data. The second section includes salary information for the 10 nonuniversity research libraries of ARL. The third section, entitled "ARL University Libraries," reports data in Tables 7 through 25 for the "general" library system of the university ARL members, combining US and Canadian data but excluding law and medical data. The fourth section, composed of Tables 26 through 30, reports data on US ARL university library members excluding law and medical data. The fifth section (Tables 31–34) reports data on Canadian ARL university libraries excluding law and medical data. The sixth section (Tables 35–41) and the seventh section (Tables 42–48) report on medical and law libraries, respectively, combining US and Canadian data.

The university population is generally treated in three distinct groups: staff in the "general" library system, staff in the university medical libraries, and staff in the university law libraries. Any branch libraries for which data were received, other than law and medical, are included in the "general" category, whether or not those libraries are administratively independent. Footnotes for many institutions provide information on branch inclusion or exclusion.

In all tables where data from US and Canadian institutions are combined, Canadian salaries are converted into US dollar equivalents at the rate of 1.0556 Canadian dollars per US dollar.[1] Tables 4 and 31 through 34, however, pertain exclusively to staff in Canadian university libraries, so salary data in those tables are expressed in Canadian dollars.

---

1 This is the average monthly noon exchange rate published in the *Bank of Canada Review* for the period July 2009–June 2010 and is used in converting figures that are shown effective as of 1 July 2010. This information can be accessed at: http://www.bankofcanada.ca/en/rates/exchange.html.

## RACE AND ETHNICITY

There were 1,266 minority professional staff reported in 99 US ARL university libraries, including law and medical libraries.[2] Note that the data for minority professionals comes only from the US ARL university libraries following the Equal Employment Opportunity Commission (EEOC) definitions; Canadian law prohibits the identification of Canadians by ethnic category.

Currently, 14.2% of the professional staff in US ARL university libraries (including law and medical libraries) belong to one of the four non-Caucasian categories for which ARL keeps records. The percentage of minorities in managerial or leadership positions in the largest US academic libraries is far lower: 6.4% are directors (7 out of 110), 6.5% are associate directors (21 out of 325), 7.7% are assistant directors (13 out of 168), and 9.1% (41 out of 452) are the head of a branch library (see Table 27). Figure 1, below, depicts the overall racial/ethnic distribution of professional staff in US ARL university libraries: Caucasian/Other 85.8%, Asian/Pacific Islander 6.6%, Black 4.4%, Hispanic 2.8%, and American Indian/Alaskan Native 0.4%.

**Figure 1: Ethnicity/Race of Professional Staff in US ARL University Libraries, FY 2010–2011**

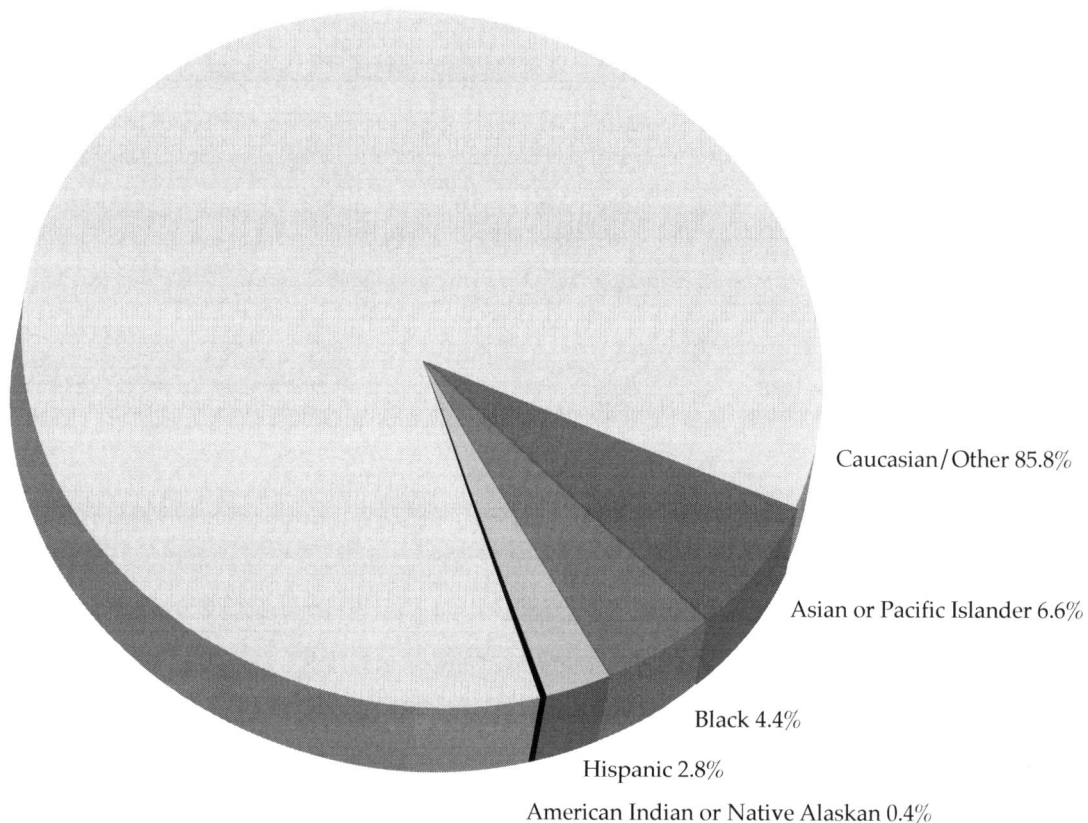

Caucasian/Other 85.8%

Asian or Pacific Islander 6.6%

Black 4.4%

Hispanic 2.8%

American Indian or Native Alaskan 0.4%

2 Some US institutions offer their librarians the option of not reporting race and ethnicity; others forbid the tracking of racial and ethnic classification altogether. See Footnotes.

Minority professional staff in US ARL university libraries continues to be disproportionately distributed across the country. Using Figure 2, we can compare the number of minority staff with other staff, region by region. These patterns of distribution have been relatively stable for the entire history of ARL's data-collection experience. Minorities are underrepresented by over 34% in the East South Central region and by more than 28% in the West North Central region (see Table 25 for a definition of the regions). Proportionately to other regions, there are more minorities in the Pacific, South Atlantic, West South Central, and Middle Atlantic regions.

**Figure 2: Minority Professionals by Region in US ARL University Libraries, FY 2010–2011**

| | New England | Middle Atlantic | East North Central | West North Central | South Atlantic | East South Central | West South Central | Mountain | Pacific | TOTAL | % |
|---|---|---|---|---|---|---|---|---|---|---|---|
| **Race/Ethnicity Category** | | | | | | | | | | | |
| **Black** | 31 | 72 | 74 | 24 | 109 | 22 | 28 | 7 | 28 | 395 | 31% |
| **Hispanic** | 21 | 44 | 27 | 10 | 39 | 6 | 40 | 20 | 43 | 250 | 20% |
| **Asian** | 79 | 105 | 69 | 25 | 84 | 9 | 40 | 21 | 155 | 587 | 46% |
| **AI/AN\*** | 3 | 3 | 15 | 4 | 1 | 0 | 1 | 7 | 0 | 34 | 3% |
| **Minority Total** | 134 | 224 | 185 | 63 | 233 | 37 | 109 | 55 | 226 | 1,266 | 100% |
| **Minority Percent** | 10.60% | 17.70% | 14.60% | 5.00% | 18.40% | 2.90% | 8.60% | 4.30% | 17.90% | | |
| **Nonminority Total** | 1,100 | 1,267 | 1,390 | 531 | 1,216 | 342 | 591 | 430 | 778 | 7,645 | 100% |
| **Nonminority Percent** | 14.40% | 16.60% | 18.20% | 6.90% | 15.90% | 4.50% | 7.70% | 5.60% | 10.20% | | |
| **Regional Percent Total staff** | 13.80% | 16.70% | 17.70% | 6.70% | 16.30% | 4.30% | 7.90% | 5.40% | 11.30% | | |
| **Proportional Minority Representation** | -26.44% | 6.76% | -19.63% | -28.35% | 15.71% | -34.67% | 11.37% | -22.76% | 75.42% | | |

\* American Indian/Alaskan Native

According to Figure 3 below, 68.6% of female professional staff in US ARL university libraries are members of the four racial/ethnic groups in Figure 2, whereas 62.4% of female professional staff are members of the Caucasian/Other racial/ethnic group. The overall gender balance in the 115 Canadian and US university libraries (including law and medical libraries) is 35.9% male and 64.1% female. See Figure 2, above, and Figure 3, below, for more detail on race/ethnic and gender distribution.

**Figure 3: Race/Ethnicity and Sex Distribution of Professional Staff in ARL University Libraries, FY 2010–2011**

| UNITED STATES | | | | | |
| --- | --- | --- | --- | --- | --- |
| | Men | | Women | | Total |
| | Number of Staff | Percent of Total | Number of Staff | Percent of Total | |
| Main | 2,785 | 37.8% | 4,587 | 62.2% | 7,372 |
| Medical | 257 | 29.7% | 608 | 70.3% | 865 |
| Law | 231 | 33.6% | 457 | 66.4% | 688 |
| Minority* | 397 | 31.4% | 869 | 68.6% | 1,266 |
| Non-minority | 2,871 | 37.6% | 4,774 | 62.4% | 7,645 |
| All | 3,268 | 36.7% | 5,643 | 63.3% | 8,911 |
| CANADA | | | | | |
| | Men | | Women | | Total |
| | Number of Staff | Percent of Total | Number of Staff | Percent of Total | |
| Main | 306 | 32.0% | 651 | 68.0% | 957 |
| Medical | 10 | 9.2% | 99 | 90.8% | 109 |
| Law | 15 | 32.6% | 31 | 67.4% | 46 |
| All | 331 | 29.8% | 781 | 70.2% | 1,112 |
| UNITED STATES AND CANADA (COMBINED) | | | | | |
| | Men | | Women | | Total |
| | Number of Staff | Percent of Total | Number of Staff | Percent of Total | |
| Main | 3,091 | 37.1% | 5,238 | 62.9% | 8,329 |
| Medical | 267 | 27.4% | 707 | 72.6% | 974 |
| Law | 246 | 33.5% | 488 | 66.5% | 734 |
| All | 3,604 | 35.9% | 6,433 | 64.1% | 10,037 |

* Includes staff in medical and law libraries.

Note: There are two US institutions that did not report race/ethnicity data; therefore, the totals will not aggregate to the total needed for the US and Canadian sub-totals to equal the figure displayed in the combined total.

ARL recognizes the difficulties that the profession has in attracting a diverse workforce and continues to work actively in the development of workplace climates that embrace diversity. The ARL Diversity Programs, through its Leadership and Career Development Program and the Initiative to Recruit a Diverse Workforce, emphasize ARL's and its members' commitment to creating a diverse academic and research library community to better meet the new challenges of global competition and changing demographics. Further, the Diversity Programs focus on issues surrounding work relationships in libraries while considering the impact of diversity on library services, interactions with library users, and the development of collections. More information about the Diversity Programs can be found at http://www.arl.org/diversity/.

ClimateQUAL® is an assessment initiative that focuses on some of the same issues. It is the Statistics and Measurement program's tool that assesses organizational climate and diversity in libraries. ClimateQUAL® helps libraries plumb the dimensions of climate and organizational culture important for a healthy organization in a library setting. The ClimateQUAL® survey addresses climate issues such as diversity, teamwork, learning, and fairness, as well as current managerial practices, and staff attitudes and beliefs. Libraries use their ClimateQUAL® data to improve their organizational climate and diversity culture for delivering superior services to the communities they serve. More information about ClimateQUAL® can be found at http://www.climatequal.org.

## GENDER DATA

Many readers of previous surveys have inquired about evidence of gender-based salary differentials in ARL libraries. Additionally, data on salary comparisons for directors also are frequently requested. Since 2008–2009, the average salary for female directors was slightly higher than that of their male counterparts. However, this year the trend was reversed, with male directors earning more than female directors (see Table 17); furthermore, the number of women in the top administrative library position decreased to 66 out of 110 total director positions reported in 2010–2011 (see Table 17).

In keeping with previous years, the 2010–2011 data show that salaries for women in US ARL university libraries have not yet met parity with that of men (see Table 17). In 2010–2011 the overall salary for women was only 96.05% of that of men for the 110 ARL university libraries (compared to 96.3% in 2009–2010). This suggests a slight regression in the slow, long-term trend towards closure of the gender gap in ARL libraries — in 1980–1981, women in ARL libraries made roughly 87% that of men.

Table 17 displays 27 job categories; females earn more than their male counterparts in just 12 of the 27 categories listed. Table 18 provides average years of professional experience for many of the same staffing categories for which salary data are shown in Table 17, revealing that experience differentials may explain some differences within specific job categories. Women have more experience in all but two of the twelve job categories in which they average higher pay. However, there are four other categories in which women, on average, have more experience and less pay: Director, Assistant Director, Department Head-Documents and Maps, and Department Head-Other. Table 19 further reveals that the average salary for men is consistently higher than the average salary for women in all ten experience cohorts. Among minority librarians, the average salary for minority men is higher than that for minority women in eight of the ten experience cohorts (see Table 30).

There is a sense that the gender gap persists in academe in areas beyond the library and that a renewed commitment to resolve the problem is needed.[3] A variety of reasons have been offered as to why these trends persist, most notably the perception that work is peripheral in a woman's life and, consequently, female-dominated professions are undervalued. Librarianship is predominantly and persistently a woman's profession.

3 There are many instances citing the continuation of gender inequity in academia. See, for example: Mary Ann Mason, "Still Earning Less," *Chronicle of Higher Education* 13 January 2010 http://chronicle.com/article/Still-Earning-Less/63482/; Katherine Mangan, "Women in Academic Medicine: Equal to Men, Except in Pay," *Chronicle of Higher Education* 31 March 2010 http://chronicle.com/article/Women-in-Academic-Medicine-/64892/; Paula Wasley, "Gender Gap in Pay Widens Over Time," *Chronicle of Higher Education* 4 May 2007 http://chronicle.com/article/Gender-Gap-in-Pay-Widens-Over/9208/; Denise K. Manger's articles in the *Chronicle of Higher Education*, "Faculty Salaries Increased 3.7% in 1999–2000" (14 April 2000: A20) and "Faculty Salaries are Up 3.6%, Double the Rate of Inflation" (23 April 1999: A16); D. W. Miller, "Salary Gap Between Male and Female Professors Grows Over the Years, Study Suggests," *Chronicle of Higher Education*, Today's News, 27 April 2000; and Yolanda Moses, "Salaries in Academe: The Gender Gap Persists," *Chronicle of Higher Education* 12 December 1997: A60.

The scarcity of men in the profession has been well documented in many studies—the largest percentage of men employed in ARL libraries was 38.2% in 1980–1981; since then men have consistently represented about 35% of the professional staff in ARL libraries.

## THE FUNCTIONAL SPECIALIST BREAKDOWN

In 2004, the ARL Statistics and Measurement Committee accepted a proposal from the ACRL Personnel Administrators and Staff Development Officers Discussion Group to break down the Functional Specialist category (FSPEC). The group's major concern was that so many different types of positions, with their varying job descriptions and salaries, were being labeled with the code FSPEC that data reported for the category were beginning to lose meaning. For each position that would have been labeled FSPEC in past years, the proposal offered ARL institutions two options: either use one of eight new codes to describe that position; or, if none of the eight new codes could adequately describe that position, use FSPEC. As seen in Figure 4, 17.3% of Functional Specialists in all libraries did not use an alternative code, an increase over the 2009–2010 figures. As in 2009–2010, Archivists and Information Technology specialists comprised the largest percentage of Functional Specialists who used an alternative code (61.5%).

**Figure 4: Distribution of Functional Specialist Job Sub-Codes by Type of Library**

| Position | Main | | Medical | | Law | | All | |
|---|---|---|---|---|---|---|---|---|
| | No. | Percent | No. | Percent | No. | Percent | No. | Percent |
| Archivists | 476 | 22.3% | 20 | 10.9% | 6 | 11.1% | 502 | 21.1% |
| Business Manager | 148 | 6.9% | 17 | 9.2% | 2 | 3.7% | 167 | 7.0% |
| Human Resources | 83 | 3.9% | 1 | 0.5% | 0 | 0.0% | 84 | 3.5% |
| IT, Systems | 397 | 18.6% | 44 | 23.9% | 13 | 24.1% | 454 | 19.1% |
| IT, Web Developer | 153 | 7.2% | 18 | 9.8% | 9 | 16.7% | 180 | 7.6% |
| IT, Programmer | 294 | 13.8% | 32 | 17.4% | 0 | 0.0% | 326 | 13.7% |
| Media Specialist | 108 | 5.1% | 7 | 3.8% | 4 | 7.4% | 116 | 4.9% |
| Preservation | 129 | 6.0% | 3 | 1.6% | 1 | 1.9% | 133 | 5.6% |
| Other Functional Specialists | 350 | 16.4% | 42 | 22.8% | 19 | 35.2% | 411 | 17.3% |
| **Total** | **2,138** | | **184** | | **54** | | **2,376** | |

Figure 5, below, displays the average salaries of the subcategories by position and sex (law and medical libraries not included) in the same fashion as Table 17. The salaries in each of the sub-categories deviate widely from the combined Functional Specialist average salary of $65,562. Human resource specialists have the highest average of all subcategories, with an average salary of $74,293; media/multimedia specialists have the lowest average salary of $56,656.

**Figure 5: Distribution of Functional Specialist Job Sub-Codes' Average Salaries by Sex**

| Position | Women | | Men | | Total | |
|---|---|---|---|---|---|---|
| | Salary | No. | Salary | No. | Salary | No. |
| Archivists | 58,579 | 304 | 62,798 | 172 | 60,103 | 476 |
| Business Manager | 71,545 | 94 | 69,483 | 54 | 70,793 | 148 |
| Human Resources | 73,821 | 70 | 76,836 | 13 | 74,293 | 83 |
| IT, Systems | 67,504 | 134 | 67,104 | 263 | 67,239 | 397 |
| IT, Web Developer | 63,210 | 65 | 65,032 | 88 | 64,258 | 153 |
| IT, Programmer | 66,506 | 91 | 69,418 | 203 | 68,516 | 294 |
| Media Specialist | 56,837 | 51 | 56,495 | 57 | 56,656 | 108 |
| Preservation | 63,646 | 89 | 66,466 | 40 | 64,521 | 129 |
| Other Functional Specialists | 63,264 | 233 | 64,515 | 117 | 63,682 | 350 |
| **All Functional Specialists** | **64,990** | **1,131** | **66,461** | **1,007** | **65,562** | **2,138** |

In regards to the gender gap in ARL libraries discussed in the previous section, it is worth noting that the average salaries of men are higher than those of women in six out of the nine categories in Figure 5.

## INSTITUTIONAL CHARACTERISTICS AND SALARIES

### A. PUBLIC AND PRIVATE INSTITUTIONS

The gap between salaries paid in private US ARL university libraries and those paid in publicly supported US university libraries increased in 2010–2011 to 7.1%, with librarians at private institutions earning an average of $4,921 more than their peers at public institutions. Out of 18 job categories, only in two (Head of Serials and Head of Computer Systems) did librarians in public institutions earn more than their peers employed in private institutions (see Table 21).

### B. LIBRARY SIZE

Library size, as measured by the number of professional staff, is another significant determinant of salary. As a rule, the largest libraries tend to pay the highest average salaries, not only overall, but for specific positions, as well. However, in 2010–2011, the libraries with between 75 and 110 staff reported the highest average salary, $74,158, followed by the largest libraries, i.e., those with more than 110 staff, which reported the next highest average salary, $73,863 (see Table 23). The gap between the highest paying cohort and the lowest paying cohort decreased in 2010–2011 to $3,994. The cutoff staffing levels used to determine the largest cohort of libraries, after declining in every year since 1995–1996, continued to hold steady at 110 in 2010–2011.[4]

### C. GEOGRAPHIC AREA

In 2010–2011, the highest average salaries were found in Canada ($83,424) followed by New England ($77,452) with salaries in the Pacific region ($75,823) coming in third (see Table 25). The Canadian average salary has

---

4 In 1995–1996, the largest cohort of libraries was determined based on staff over 124; in 1996–1998, over 120; in 1998-1999, over 115; and since 1999–2000, over 110. See Table 23.

not been this high since 2008–2009 when it was $82,295. This sharp increase in Canadian salaries is due to fluctuations in the currency exchange rate. For the 2010–2011 survey period the Canadian currency exchange rate is 1.0556. The East South Central region had the lowest average salary: $62,842.

## D. Rank Structure

Rank structure provides a useful framework for examining professional salaries in ARL university libraries. Figure 6, below, displays average salary and years of experience in the most commonly used rank structures. Readers should be aware that not all individuals have a rank that fits into the rank structure the library utilizes. Most commonly, directors may have no rank (or a rank outside the structure) and it is common for non-librarians included in the survey (business officers, personnel staff, computer specialists, liaisons, etc.) to be unranked, as well.

The pattern of relationships between rank and salary seen in past years continues: with higher rank associated with higher average years of experience and a correspondingly higher salary. 5,722 of the 8,329 librarians in ARL university member libraries occupy a rank within these three most commonly found ranking systems, and the largest number of professionals (3,183) occupy a position in a four-step rank structure.

**Figure 6: Average Salaries and Average Years of Experience of Library Professionals in Libraries with Three, Four, and Five Step Rank Structures, FY 2010–2011**

|  | Three-Step | | Four-Step | | Five-Step | |
|---|---|---|---|---|---|---|
|  | Salary | Experience | Salary | Experience | Salary | Experience |
| Librarian 1 | 59,888 | 9.2 | 53,813 | 7.9 | 53,176 | 7.7 |
| Librarian 2 | 69,935 | 17.6 | 60,214 | 13.1 | 59,922 | 13.0 |
| Librarian 3 | 87,641 | 25.4 | 72,896 | 20.4 | 68,968 | 17.5 |
| Librarian 4 |  |  | 88,116 | 26.3 | 87,744 | 23.6 |
| Librarian 5 |  |  |  |  | 103,069 | 29.1 |
| **No. of Staff** | **1,475** | | **3,183** | | **1,064** | |

## Inflation Effect

Tables 2 and 6 reveal changes in beginning professional and median salaries as reported by both university and nonuniversity research libraries as well as the US Bureau of Labor's Cost of Living Index (CPI-All Urban Consumers). Table 3 is similar to Table 2, but reports data only on US libraries. Table 4 shows trend data for Canadian libraries and compares them to the changes in the Canadian Consumer Price Index (Consumer Price Index for Canada, all-items, not seasonally adjusted). Tables 2, 3, and 4 include law and medical library staff in ARL university libraries. In contrast to 2009–2010, these tables indicate that the purchasing power of professionals (in both the United States and Canada) employed in ARL libraries kept pace with inflation.

The median salary for US ARL university libraries in 2010 increased to $65,000 (see Table 3). This modest salary increase barely kept pace with the rebounding economy, which saw the US CPI increase by 1.2% (see Table 3).[5] Likewise, Canadian salaries (reported in Canadian dollars) also barely surpassed inflation: the Canadian CPI

5 CPI data retrieved from the US Department of Labor, Bureau of Labor Statistics' *Consumer Price Index-All Urban Consumers (US All items, 1982-84=100 - CUUR0000SA0)* available online at http://www.bls.gov/data/.

increased 1.8%, while median salaries in Canadian university libraries increased to $82,251(Canadian dollars, see Table 4).[6] The sharp difference in the exchange rates between 2009–2010 (1.1667 Canadian per US dollar) and 2010–2011 (1.0556 Canadian per US dollar) contributed to these changes.

The median beginning salary (BPS) for university ARL librarians rebounded back to 2008–2009 levels to $44,004 in 2010–2011 (see Table 2). Table 6 shows that nonuniversity librarians also experienced increases in their median and beginning salaries in 2010–2011, which increased to $95,020 and $51,135, respectively.

Readers are reminded that these data reflect only salaries, and that there are other compensation issues which may have influenced the pattern of salaries in various institutions. In addition, a highly standardized structure for capturing data has been used, which may portray results in a way that cannot be fully representative of a local situation.

Martha Kyrillidou
Shaneka Morris
Association of Research Libraries
September 30, 2011

---

6 The source for Canadian CPI data is *Table 5: The Consumer Price Index for Canada (All-Items, Not Seasonally Adjusted, Historical Data)* published in *The Daily*, a Statistics Canada publication, available online at http://www.statcan.gc.ca/pub/62-001-x/2009010/t040-eng.htm.

# SALARY LEVELS FOR STAFF IN ARL LIBRARIES

## TABLES 1–4

# TABLE 1: DISTRIBUTION BY SALARY LEVEL

Figures in columns headed by fiscal year show the number of filled professional positions. Columns headed by Cum. % show the percentage of all filled positions with salaries equal to or more than the beginning of each salary range.

Note: Canadian salaries are expressed in US dollars. Data includes medical and law libraries.

| Salary Range | University Libraries | | | | Nonuniversity Libraries | | | |
|---|---|---|---|---|---|---|---|---|
| | FY 2009–2010 | Cum. % | FY 2010–2011 | Cum. % | FY 2009–2010 | Cum. % | FY 2010–2011 | Cum. % |
| 300,000 and above | 6 | 0.1% | 6 | 0.1% | 0 | 0.0% | 0 | 0.0% |
| 250,000–299,999 | 12 | 0.2% | 11 | 0.2% | 1 | 0.0% | 0 | 0.0% |
| 200,000–250,000 | 37 | 0.5% | 42 | 0.6% | 3 | 0.1% | 3 | 0.1% |
| 175,000–199,999 | 58 | 1.1% | 56 | 1.1% | 6 | 0.3% | 7 | 0.3% |
| 150,000–174,999 | 80 | 1.9% | 87 | 2.0% | 284 | 7.7% | 315 | 8.8% |
| 140,000–149,999 | 52 | 2.4% | 70 | 2.7% | 105 | 10.5% | 116 | 11.9% |
| 130,000–139,999 | 80 | 3.2% | 99 | 3.7% | 237 | 16.7% | 218 | 17.8% |
| 120,000–129,999 | 127 | 4.4% | 141 | 5.1% | 170 | 21.1% | 252 | 24.6% |
| 110,000–119,999 | 193 | 6.3% | 253 | 7.6% | 370 | 30.9% | 331 | 33.5% |
| 100,000–109,999 | 328 | 9.5% | 402 | 11.6% | 383 | 40.9% | 422 | 44.9% |
| 95,000–99,999 | 287 | 12.3% | 304 | 14.7% | 301 | 48.8% | 205 | 50.4% |
| 90,000–94,999 | 337 | 15.6% | 312 | 17.8% | 144 | 52.6% | 210 | 56.1% |
| 85,000–89,999 | 418 | 19.7% | 452 | 22.3% | 276 | 59.8% | 206 | 61.6% |
| 80,000–84,999 | 546 | 25.1% | 575 | 28.0% | 201 | 65.1% | 241 | 68.1% |
| 79,000–79,999 | 121 | 26.3% | 122 | 29.2% | 48 | 66.4% | 63 | 69.8% |
| 78,000–78,999 | 143 | 27.7% | 118 | 30.4% | 48 | 67.6% | 5 | 69.9% |
| 76,000–77,999 | 261 | 30.2% | 258 | 33.0% | 49 | 68.9% | 66 | 71.7% |
| 74,000–75,999 | 321 | 33.4% | 320 | 36.1% | 89 | 71.2% | 115 | 74.8% |
| 72,000–73,999 | 285 | 36.2% | 338 | 39.5% | 123 | 74.5% | 56 | 76.3% |
| 70,000–71,999 | 323 | 39.3% | 351 | 43.0% | 29 | 75.2% | 83 | 78.6% |
| 68,000–69,999 | 400 | 43.3% | 387 | 46.9% | 97 | 77.8% | 94 | 81.1% |
| 66,000–67,999 | 370 | 46.9% | 374 | 50.6% | 89 | 80.1% | 79 | 83.2% |
| 64,000–65,999 | 451 | 51.3% | 480 | 55.4% | 89 | 82.4% | 49 | 84.6% |
| 62,000–63,999 | 400 | 55.2% | 377 | 59.1% | 114 | 85.4% | 178 | 89.4% |
| 60,000–61,999 | 530 | 60.4% | 495 | 64.1% | 93 | 87.9% | 47 | 90.6% |
| 58,000–59,999 | 430 | 64.6% | 408 | 68.1% | 46 | 89.1% | 54 | 92.1% |
| 56,000–57,999 | 487 | 69.4% | 457 | 72.7% | 120 | 92.2% | 61 | 93.7% |
| 54,000–55,999 | 459 | 73.9% | 422 | 76.9% | 44 | 93.4% | 48 | 95.0% |
| 52,000–53,999 | 496 | 78.7% | 476 | 81.6% | 84 | 95.6% | 45 | 96.2% |
| 50,000–51,999 | 439 | 83.1% | 397 | 85.6% | 87 | 97.9% | 75 | 98.2% |
| 48,000–49,999 | 446 | 87.4% | 353 | 89.1% | 13 | 98.2% | 10 | 98.5% |
| 46,000–47,999 | 368 | 91.0% | 330 | 92.4% | 16 | 98.6% | 7 | 98.7% |
| 44,000–45,999 | 326 | 94.2% | 263 | 95.0% | 11 | 98.9% | 8 | 98.9% |
| 42,000–43,999 | 217 | 96.3% | 200 | 97.0% | 14 | 99.3% | 33 | 99.8% |
| 40,000–41,999 | 175 | 98.1% | 134 | 98.3% | 17 | 99.7% | 0 | 99.8% |
| 38,000–39,999 | 85 | 98.9% | 67 | 99.0% | 0 | 99.7% | 1 | 99.8% |
| 36,000–37,999 | 52 | 99.4% | 39 | 99.4% | 2 | 99.8% | 2 | 99.9% |
| 34,000–35,999 | 38 | 99.8% | 25 | 99.6% | 3 | 99.9% | 2 | 99.9% |
| less than 34,000 | 23 | 100.0% | 36 | 100.0% | 5 | 100.0% | 2 | 100.0% |
| **Total Positions** | **10,207** | | **10,037** | | **3,748** | | **3,709** | |
| **Median Salary** | **$64,560** | | **$66,260** | | **$80,320** | | **$95,020** | |

## TABLE 2: SALARY TRENDS IN ARL UNIVERSITY LIBRARIES

Salary figures for the current year are displayed in the context of previous years and compared to the changes in the US Consumer Price Index (CPI) to show trends in the purchasing power of median and beginning professional salaries. Salary figures and CPI numbers have been converted to adjusted indexes, using July 1984 as the base. Actual CPI data retrieved from the US Department of Labor, Bureau of Labor Statistics' *Consumer Price Index-All Urban Consumers (US All items, 1982–1984=100 - CUUR0000SA0)* available online at http://www.bls.gov/data/.

Note: Canadian salaries are expressed in US dollars.

| Fiscal Year | Number of Libraries | Total Staff | Median Salary† | BPS‡ Median | Median Salary Index | BPS‡ Index | Actual CPI* | Adjusted CPI |
|---|---|---|---|---|---|---|---|---|
| 2010–2011 | 115 | 10,037 | $66,260 | $44,004 | 253.9 | 266.7 | 218.0 | 209.8 |
| 2009–2010 | 114 | 10,207 | 64,560 | 43,700 | 247.4 | 264.8 | 215.4 | 207.3 |
| 2008–2009 | 113 | 10,148 | 64,823 | 44,000 | 248.4 | 266.7 | 219.9 | 211.6 |
| 2007–2008 | 113 | 9,983 | 61,833 | 41,125 | 236.9 | 249.7 | 208.3 | 200.5 |
| 2006–2007 | 113 | 9,824 | 59,648 | 40,000 | 228.5 | 242.4 | 203.5 | 195.9 |
| 2005–2006 | 113 | 9,655 | 57,074 | 37,920 | 218.7 | 229.8 | 195.4 | 188.1 |
| 2004–2005 | 113 | 9,487 | 55,250 | 36,984 | 211.7 | 224.1 | 189.4 | 182.3 |
| 2003–2004 | 114 | 9,492 | 53,000 | 36,000 | 203.1 | 218.2 | 183.9 | 177.0 |
| 2002–2003 | 114 | 9,469 | 51,636 | 35,000 | 197.8 | 212.1 | 180.1 | 173.3 |
| 2001–2002 | 113 | 9,198 | 50,724 | 34,000 | 194.3 | 206.1 | 177.5 | 170.8 |
| 2000–2001 | 112 | 8,882 | 49,068 | 32,879 | 188.0 | 199.3 | 172.8 | 166.3 |
| 1999-2000 | 111 | 8,595 | 47,377 | 31,100 | 181.5 | 188.5 | 166.7 | 160.4 |
| 1998–1999 | 110 | 8,400 | 45,775 | 30,000 | 175.2 | 181.7 | 163.2 | 157.1 |
| 1997–1998 | 110 | 8,414 | 44,534 | 28,500 | 170.5 | 172.6 | 160.5 | 154.5 |
| 1996–1997 | 109 | 8,325 | 43,170 | 27,687 | 165.3 | 167.7 | 157.0 | 151.1 |
| 1995–1996 | 108 | 8,231 | 41,901 | 27,000 | 160.5 | 163.6 | 152.5 | 146.8 |
| 1994–1995 | 108 | 8,216 | 41,088 | 26,000 | 157.4 | 157.6 | 148.4 | 142.8 |
| 1993–1994 | 108 | 8,132 | 40,225 | 25,834 | 154.1 | 156.6 | 144.4 | 139.0 |
| 1992–1993 | 108 | 8,212 | 39,265 | 25,000 | 150.4 | 151.5 | 140.5 | 134.9 |
| 1991–1992 | 107 | 8,256 | 38,537 | 24,000 | 147.7 | 145.5 | 136.2 | 131.1 |
| 1990–1991 | 107 | 8,382 | 36,701 | 23,800 | 140.6 | 144.2 | 130.4 | 125.8 |
| 1989–1990 | 107 | 8,253 | 34,629 | 22,000 | 132.7 | 133.3 | 124.4 | 119.3 |
| 1988–1989 | 107 | 8,087 | 32,461 | 20,400 | 124.4 | 123.6 | 118.5 | 113.9 |
| 1987–1988 | 106 | 7,962 | 30,534 | 19,460 | 117.0 | 117.9 | 113.8 | 109.3 |
| 1986–1987 | 105 | 7,718 | 28,941 | 18,250 | 110.9 | 110.6 | 109.5 | 105.5 |
| 1985–1986 | 105 | 7,543 | 27,485 | 17,500 | 105.3 | 106.1 | 107.8 | 103.6 |
| 1984–1985 | 104 | 7,161 | 26,100 | 16,500 | 100.0 | 100.0 | 104.1 | 100.0 |

*Actual CPI figures have been revised from previous editions based upon changes published by the Bureau of Labor Statistics. These changes are minute, less than 0.3 in all cases.
† Includes medical and law libraries.
‡ Beginning professional salary.

## TABLE 3: SALARY TRENDS IN US ARL UNIVERSITY LIBRARIES

Salary figures for the current year are displayed in the context of previous years and compared to the changes in the US Consumer Price Index (CPI) to show trends in the purchasing power of median and beginning professional salaries. Salary figures and CPI numbers have been converted to adjusted indexes, using July 1984 as the base. Actual CPI data retrieved from the US Department of Labor, Bureau of Labor Statistics' *Consumer Price Index-All Urban Consumers (US All items, 1982–1984=100 - CUUR0000SA0)* available online at http://www.bls.gov/data/.

| Fiscal Year | Number of Libraries | Total Staff | Median Salary† | Median Salary Change | Median Salary Index | Actual CPI* | Adjusted CPI | CPI Change |
|---|---|---|---|---|---|---|---|---|
| 2010–2011 | 99 | 8,925 | $65,000 | 1.5% | 250.5 | 218.0 | 209.8 | 1.2% |
| 2009–2010 | 99 | 9,116 | 64,069 | 0.6 | 246.9 | 215.4 | 207.3 | -2.0 |
| 2008–2009 | 99 | 9,158 | 63,673 | 3.8 | 245.4 | 219.9 | 211.6 | 5.6 |
| 2007–2008 | 99 | 9,026 | 61,329 | 3.5 | 236.4 | 208.3 | 200.5 | 2.4 |
| 2006–2007 | 99 | 8,866 | 59,280 | 3.7 | 228.5 | 203.5 | 195.9 | 4.1 |
| 2005–2006 | 99 | 8,700 | 57,173 | 2.8 | 220.4 | 195.4 | 188.1 | 3.2 |
| 2004–2005 | 99 | 8,581 | 55,600 | 3.2 | 214.3 | 189.4 | 182.3 | 3.0 |
| 2003–2004 | 100 | 8,581 | 53,859 | 2.0 | 207.6 | 183.9 | 177.0 | 2.1 |
| 2002–2003 | 100 | 8,544 | 52,789 | 1.9 | 203.5 | 180.1 | 173.3 | 1.5 |
| 2001–2002 | 99 | 8,337 | 51,806 | 4.1 | 199.7 | 177.5 | 170.8 | 2.7 |
| 2000–2001 | 99 | 8,127 | 49,753 | 3.7 | 191.8 | 172.8 | 166.3 | 3.7 |
| 1999-2000 | 98 | 7,858 | 48,000 | 4.1 | 185.0 | 166.7 | 160.4 | 2.1 |
| 1998–1999 | 97 | 7,671 | 46,130 | 3.6 | 177.8 | 163.2 | 157.1 | 1.7 |
| 1997–1998 | 97 | 7,682 | 44,544 | 3.4 | 171.7 | 160.5 | 154.5 | 2.2 |
| 1996–1997 | 96 | 7,562 | 43,084 | 3.4 | 166.1 | 157.0 | 151.1 | 3.0 |
| 1995–1996 | 95 | 7,435 | 41,651 | 2.7 | 160.5 | 152.5 | 146.8 | 2.8 |
| 1994–1995 | 95 | 7,401 | 40,573 | 3.4 | 156.4 | 148.4 | 142.8 | 2.8 |
| 1993–1994 | 95 | 7,390 | 39,257 | 3.0 | 151.3 | 144.4 | 139.0 | 2.8 |
| 1992–1993 | 95 | 7,375 | 38,124 | 3.0 | 146.9 | 140.5 | 134.9 | 3.2 |
| 1991–1992 | 94 | 7,408 | 37,009 | 3.5 | 142.6 | 136.2 | 131.1 | 4.4 |
| 1990–1991 | 94 | 7,543 | 35,761 | 5.2 | 137.8 | 130.4 | 125.8 | 4.8 |
| 1989–1990 | 94 | 7,344 | 34,000 | 5.8 | 131.0 | 124.4 | 119.3 | 5.0 |
| 1988–1989 | 94 | 7,252 | 32,149 | 5.4 | 123.9 | 118.5 | 113.9 | 4.1 |
| 1987–1988 | 93 | 7,145 | 30,492 | 5.1 | 117.5 | 113.8 | 109.3 | 3.9 |
| 1986–1987 | 92 | 6,886 | 29,021 | 6.5 | 111.9 | 109.5 | 105.5 | 1.6 |
| 1985–1986 | 91 | 6,707 | 27,249 | 5.0 | 105.0 | 107.8 | 103.6 | 3.6 |
| 1984–1985 | 91 | 6,456 | 25,946 | 6.9 | 100.0 | 104.1 | 100.0 | - |

*Actual CPI figures have been revised from previous editions based upon changes published by the Bureau of Labor Statistics. These changes are minute, less than 0.3 in all cases.
† Includes medical and law libraries.

## TABLE 4: SALARY TRENDS IN CANADIAN ARL UNIVERSITY LIBRARIES

Salary figures for the current year are displayed in the context of previous years. Canadian salaries are presented in both US $ and Canadian $ denominations and the annual exchange rate used in the salary surveys is also listed. Canadian salaries are also compared to the changes in the Canadian Consumer Price Index (CPI) to show trends in the purchasing power of median Canadian salaries. CPI number changes are based on July CPI figures. The source for Canadian CPI data is "Table 5: The Consumer Price Index for Canada" published in *The Daily*, a Statistics Canada publication, available online at http://www.statcan.gc.ca/pub/62-001-x/2011004/t040-eng.htm.

| Fiscal Year | Number of Libraries | Total Staff | Median Salary in US $† | Median Salary Change† | Exchange Rate | Median Salary in Can. $ | Median Salary Change | Can. CPI** | Can. CPI Change* |
|---|---|---|---|---|---|---|---|---|---|
| 2010–2011 | 16 | 1,112 | $77,919 | 12.7% | 1.0556 | $82,251 | 2.0% | 116.8 | 1.8% |
| 2009–2010 | 15 | 1,091 | 69,130 | -11.3% | 1.1667 | 80,654 | 2.4 | 114.7 | -0.9 |
| 2008–2009 | 14 | 990 | 77,954 | 15.8 | 1.0101 | 78,742 | 3.3 | 115.8 | 3.4 |
| 2007–2008 | 14 | 957 | 67,331 | 6.7 | 1.1323 | 76,239 | 3.9 | 112.0 | 2.2 |
| 2006–2007 | 14 | 958 | 63,112 | 11.8 | 1.16289 | 73,392 | 4.0 | 109.6 | 2.3 |
| 2005–2006 | 14 | 955 | 56,474 | 7.1 | 1.24971 | 70,576 | -0.3 | 107.1 | 2.0 |
| 2004–2005 | 14 | 906 | 52,707 | 16.3 | 1.34328 | 70,800 | 3.5 | 105.0 | 2.3 |
| 2003–2004 | 14 | 911 | 45,310 | 6.2 | 1.51023 | 68,429 | 2.3 | 102.6 | 2.1 |
| 2002–2003 | 14 | 925 | 42,657 | -0.6 | 1.56878 | 66,919 | 2.6 | 100.5 | 2.1 |
| 2001–2002 | 14 | 861 | 42,928 | -1.1 | 1.51919 | 65,215 | 2.1 | 98.4 | 2.7 |
| 2000–2001 | 13 | 755 | 43,394 | 5.0 | 1.47192 | 63,873 | 2.4 | 95.8 | 2.9 |
| 1999-2000 | 13 | 737 | 41,316 | -3.8 | 1.5103 | 62,400 | 2.4 | 93.1 | 1.9 |
| 1998–1999 | 13 | 729 | 42,963 | -2.7 | 1.4177 | 60,909 | 0.9 | 91.4 | 1.0 |
| 1997–1998 | 13 | 732 | 44,167 | 1.4 | 1.3663 | 60,346 | 1.7 | 90.5 | 1.7 |
| 1996–1997 | 13 | 764 | 43,569 | 0.9 | 1.3613 | 59,310 | -0.4 | 89.0 | 1.3 |
| 1995–1996 | 13 | 796 | 43,173 | -1.7 | 1.3794 | 59,554 | 1.3 | 87.9 | 2.6 |
| 1994–1995 | 13 | 815 | 43,919 | -6.0 | 1.3381 | 58,768 | 0.7 | 85.7 | 0.1 |
| 1993–1994 | 13 | 816 | 46,744 | -4.3 | 1.2488 | 58,374 | 2.9 | 85.6 | 1.7 |
| 1992–1993 | 13 | 837 | 48,820 | 2.7 | 1.1623 | 56,744 | 3.4 | 84.2 | 1.2 |
| 1991–1992 | 13 | 847 | 47,519 | 5.5 | 1.1547 | 54,870 | 3.6 | 83.2 | 6.0 |
| 1990–1991 | 13 | 839 | 45,023 | 15.1 | 1.1759 | 52,942 | 12.5 | 78.5 | 4.1 |
| 1989–1990 | 13 | 853 | 39,117 | 12.3 | 1.2026 | 47,042 | 5.3 | 75.4 | 5.3 |
| 1988–1989 | 13 | 837 | 34,826 | 11.7 | 1.2826 | 44,668 | 5.3 | 71.6 | 3.9 |
| 1987–1988 | 13 | 817 | 31,178 | 10.9 | 1.3602 | 42,408 | 9.1 | 68.9 | 4.6 |
| 1986–1987 | 13 | 831 | 28,123 | -1.9 | 1.3817 | 38,858 | 1.2 | 65.9 | 4.1 |
| 1985–1986 | 13 | 829 | 28,666 | 1.1 | 1.3388 | 38,378 | 7.9 | 63.3 | 4.1 |
| 1984–1985 | 12 | 705 | 28,346 | -0.8 | 1.2548 | 35,569 | 0.8 | 60.8 | 4.1 |
| **Average** | | | | **3.8%** | | | **3.3%** | | |

† Includes medical and law libraries.

* Canadian CPI change figures have been revised from previous editions based upon changes published by *The Daily* (Statistics Canada). These changes were caused by rounding; they are minute and are less than 0.3 in all cases.

** Actual Canadian CPI figures have been added to this table (not available in previous editions).

# ARL Nonuniversity Libraries

## Tables 5–6

# TABLE 5: MEDIAN AND BEGINNING PROFESSIONAL SALARIES IN ARL NONUNIVERSITY LIBRARIES

| | No. of Staff | Median Salaries | | Beginning Salaries | |
|---|---|---|---|---|---|
| | | FY 2009–2010 | FY 2010–2011 | FY 2009–2010 | FY 2010–2011 |
| Boston Public Library | 167 | $67,184 | $67,267 | $40,975 | $40,975 |
| Canada Institute for Scientific and Technical Information * † | 82 | 67,639 | 73,649 | 44,446 | 53,155 |
| Center for Research Libraries | 33 | 50,799 | 52,179 | 33,878 | 33,878 |
| Library & Archives Canada * | 99 | 56,601 | 63,497 | 45,141 | 50,640 |
| Library of Congress | 2,678 | 101,416 | 103,872 | 50,408 | 51,630 |
| National Agricultural Library† | 87 | 82,845 | 84,855 | 50,408 | 51,630 |
| National Library of Medicine | 208 | 90,154 | 92,341 | 50,408 | 42,209 |
| New York Public Library | 244 | 63,696 | 61,438 | 42,638 | 42,638 |
| New York State Library | 54 | 64,305 | 68,637 | 49,968 | 53,366 |
| Smithsonian Library | 57 | 85,281 | 87,350 | 52,089 | 51,630 |

* Canadian salaries are expressed in US dollars.
† See footnotes.

## TABLE 6: SALARY TRENDS IN ARL NONUNIVERSITY LIBRARIES

Salary figures for the current year are displayed in the context of the previous years and compared to the changes in the Consumer Price Index (CPI) to show trends in the purchasing power of median and beginning professional salaries. Salary figures and CPI numbers have been converted to adjusted indexes, using July 1984 as the base. Actual CPI data retrieved from the US Department of Labor, Bureau of Labor Statistics' *Consumer Price Index-All Urban Consumers (US All items, 1982–1984=100 - CUUR0000SA0)* available online at http://www. bls.gov/data/.

Note: Canadian salaries are expressed in US dollars.

| Fiscal Year | Number of Libraries | Total Staff | Median Salary | BPS† Median | Median Salary Index | BPS† Index | Actual CPI | Adjusted CPI |
|---|---|---|---|---|---|---|---|---|
| 2010–2011 | 10 | 3,709 | $95,020 | $51,135 | 280.5 | 309.8 | 218.0 | 209.8 |
| 2009–2010 | 10 | 3,811 | 85,229 | 47,554 | 251.6 | 288.1 | 215.4 | 207.3 |
| 2008–2009 | 10 | 3,748 | 85,320 | 48,108 | 251.8 | 291.4 | 219.9 | 211.6 |
| 2007–2008 | 10 | 3,797 | 80,261 | 44,359 | 236.9 | 268.7 | 208.3 | 200.5 |
| 2006–2007 | 10 | 3,832 | 80,124 | 42,765 | 236.5 | 259.1 | 203.5 | 195.9 |
| 2005–2006 | 10 | 3,921 | 76,083 | 38,673 | 224.6 | 234.3 | 195.4 | 188.1 |
| 2004–2005 | 10 | 3,946 | 74,022 | 34,764 | 218.5 | 210.6 | 189.4 | 182.3 |
| 2003–2004 | 10 | 3,877 | 70,020 | 34,739 | 206.8 | 210.4 | 183.9 | 177.0 |
| 2002–2003 | 10 | 3,804 | 65,289 | 34,739 | 192.7 | 210.4 | 180.1 | 173.3 |
| 2001–2002 | 10 | 3,717 | 65,025 | 34,389 | 191.9 | 208.3 | 177.5 | 170.8 |
| 2000–2001 | 10 | 3,731 | 62,521 | 31,774 | 184.5 | 192.5 | 172.8 | 166.3 |
| 1999-2000 | 10 | 3,737 | 59,916 | 30,849 | 176.8 | 186.9 | 166.7 | 160.4 |
| 1998–1999 | 11 | 3,819 | 56,000 | 29,877 | 165.3 | 181.0 | 163.2 | 157.1 |
| 1997–1998 | 11 | 3,779 | 55,055 | 28,724 | 162.5 | 174.0 | 160.5 | 154.5 |
| 1996–1997 | 11 | 3,799 | 51,150 | 28,380 | 151.0 | 172.0 | 157.0 | 151.1 |
| 1995–1996 | 11 | 3,915 | 49,149 | 28,162 | 145.1 | 170.7 | 152.5 | 146.8 |
| 1994–1995 | 11 | 3,837 | 47,997 | 27,813 | 141.7 | 168.6 | 148.4 | 142.8 |
| 1993–1994 | 11 | 4,003 | 44,949 | 26,806 | 132.7 | 162.5 | 144.4 | 139.0 |
| 1992–1993 | 11 | 4,172 | 43,876 | 23,500 | 129.6 | 142.4 | 140.2 | 134.9 |
| 1991–1992 | 11 | 2,906 | 42,455 | 23,500 | 125.4 | 142.4 | 136.2 | 131.1 |
| 1990–1991 | 12 | 1,363 | 36,013 | 20,800 | 106.3 | 126.1 | 130.7 | 125.8 |
| 1989–1990 | 11 | 3,767 | 40,106 | 20,195 | 118.4 | 122.4 | 124.0 | 119.3 |
| 1988–1989 | 11 | 3,781 | 37,544 | 19,100 | 110.9 | 115.8 | 118.3 | 113.9 |
| 1987–1988 | 11 | 3,765 | 36,250 | 18,405 | 107.0 | 111.5 | 113.6 | 109.3 |
| 1986–1987 | 10 | 2,790 | 33,020 | 17,912 | 97.5 | 108.6 | 109.6 | 105.5 |
| 1985–1986 | 12 | 3,874 | 33,720 | 17,308 | 99.6 | 104.9 | 107.6 | 103.6 |
| 1984–1985 | 11 | 3,840 | 33,863 | 16,500 | 100.0 | 100.0 | 103.9 | 100.0 |

† Beginning professional salary.

# ARL University Libraries

## Tables 7–25

## TABLE 7: FILLED POSITIONS; AVERAGE, MEDIAN, AND BEGINNING SALARIES; AND AVERAGE YEARS OF EXPERIENCE IN ARL UNIVERSITY LIBRARIES, FY 2010–2011

| Institution | FILLED POSITIONS FY 2011 | AVERAGE SALARIES FY 2010 | AVERAGE SALARIES FY 2011 | MEDIAN SALARIES FY 2010 | MEDIAN SALARIES FY 2011 | BEGINNING SALARIES FY 2010 | BEGINNING SALARIES FY 2011 | AVERAGE YRS. EXP. FY 2011 |
|---|---|---|---|---|---|---|---|---|
| Alabama ‡ | 62 | $58,272 | $58,760 | $52,204 | $55,188 | $42,000 | $42,000 | 15.0 |
| Alberta †‡ | 72 | 84,172 | 96,215 | 89,319 | 96,759 | 43,398 | 52,833 | 15.7 |
| Arizona ‡ | 55 | 65,897 | 65,351 | 59,915 | 59,118 | 48,605 | 50,857 | 18.0 |
| Arizona State ‡ | 56 | 66,091 | 64,744 | 65,071 | 65,039 | 43,000 | 43,000 | 19.9 |
| Auburn ‡ | 44 | 58,382 | 57,728 | 53,705 | 52,330 | 44,720 | 44,720 | 15.1 |
| Boston University ‡ | 56 | 57,615 | 59,680 | 56,600 | 57,200 | 43,700 | 33,000 | 17.5 |
| Boston College ‡ | 55 | 69,739 | 70,871 | 67,280 | 69,560 | 42,300 | 43,350 | 19.7 |
| Brigham Young | 109 | 66,005 | 67,295 | 63,950 | 66,000 | 51,000 | 52,020 | 18.9 |
| British Columbia †‡ | 72 | 73,023 | 85,029 | 70,005 | 83,131 | 47,429 | 52,420 | 17.7 |
| Brown ‡ | 62 | 65,880 | 66,368 | 61,549 | 62,972 | 39,500 | 40,500 | 18.8 |
| Calgary †‡ | 53 | 81,275 | 91,776 | 76,749 | 88,732 | 49,713 | 54,945 | 18.7 |
| California, Berkeley ‡ | 101 | 83,853 | 85,329 | 82,524 | 82,524 | 47,087 | 46,164 | 18.0 |
| California, Davis ‡ | 39 | 81,135 | 84,334 | 88,488 | 88,488 | 46,164 | 46,164 | 21.8 |
| California, Irvine | 51 | 76,645 | 77,825 | 75,708 | 75,708 | 46,164 | 46,144 | 16.8 |
| California, Los Angeles ‡ | 136 | 78,189 | 79,113 | 75,708 | 75,708 | 46,164 | 46,164 | 16.3 |
| California, Riverside ‡ | 43 | 77,661 | 79,762 | 75,708 | 79,116 | 47,087 | 47,087 | 21.5 |
| California, San Diego ‡ | 84 | 77,158 | 77,064 | 75,708 | 75,708 | 46,164 | 46,164 | 17.4 |
| California, Santa Barbara ‡ | 55 | 71,378 | 74,431 | 68,892 | 74,104 | 46,164 | 46,164 | 17.8 |
| Case Western Reserve ‡ | 43 | 58,788 | 58,886 | 55,227 | 55,434 | 35,000 | 35,000 | 15.9 |
| Chicago ‡ | 71 | 76,254 | 76,692 | 72,329 | 73,130 | 48,204 | 50,151 | 20.8 |
| Cincinnati ‡ | 58 | 65,445 | 68,451 | 61,879 | 66,260 | 40,000 | 42,000 | 19.5 |
| Colorado ‡ | 45 | 67,523 | 64,595 | 64,573 | 61,262 | 44,000 | 44,000 | 14.2 |
| Colorado State | 37 | 68,311 | 67,844 | 65,300 | 64,700 | 45,000 | 55,000 | 18.0 |
| Columbia ‡ | 204 | 72,939 | 74,360 | 64,385 | 65,280 | 51,500 | 52,000 | 15.8 |
| Connecticut ‡ | 60 | 82,083 | 81,341 | 78,079 | 79,309 | 48,000 | 50,000 | 17.8 |
| Cornell ‡ | 102 | 71,548 | 74,377 | 64,239 | 66,873 | 47,000 | 48,000 | 17.1 |
| Dartmouth ‡ | 47 | 72,208 | 70,594 | 67,933 | 67,159 | 45,500 | 45,500 | 17.6 |
| Delaware | 59 | 75,703 | 76,673 | 73,353 | 72,868 | 43,600 | 43,600 | 18.2 |
| Duke ‡ | 117 | 64,870 | 65,526 | 60,000 | 60,000 | 45,000 | 45,000 | 15.0 |
| Emory ‡ | 67 | 68,747 | 69,761 | 63,068 | 63,198 | 42,000 | 47,750 | 15.0 |
| Florida ‡ | 68 | 60,450 | 62,229 | 56,388 | 58,073 | 42,000 | 42,000 | 16.3 |
| Florida State ‡ | 41 | 54,858 | 56,313 | 49,805 | 52,265 | 42,000 | 42,000 | 12.5 |
| George Washington ‡ | 41 | 74,353 | 76,999 | 67,143 | 72,277 | 47,000 | 47,000 | 15.9 |
| Georgetown ‡ | 53 | 69,227 | 70,338 | 63,538 | 63,965 | 45,000 | 45,000 | 21.6 |
| Georgia ‡ | 69 | 56,544 | 56,057 | 50,000 | 49,795 | 38,000 | 38,000 | 16.5 |
| Georgia Tech ‡ | 44 | 63,526 | 63,534 | 58,016 | 58,016 | 44,000 | 44,000 | 14.8 |
| Guelph †‡ | 50 | 69,113 | 80,588 | 66,902 | 76,872 | 51,169 | 58,392 | 18.1 |
| Harvard ‡ | 408 | 77,319 | 79,111 | 70,720 | 72,134 | 48,800 | 53,093 | 15.4 |
| Hawaii ‡ | 67 | 66,721 | 63,037 | 66,225 | 64,692 | 42,660 | 35,000 | 18.2 |
| Houston ‡ | 41 | 61,669 | 62,188 | 56,563 | 54,628 | 43,000 | 44,000 | 15.0 |
| Howard ‡ | 13 | 43,547 | 56,590 | 43,010 | 50,223 | 38,000 | 34,627 | 22.5 |
| Illinois, Chicago ‡ | 43 | 62,208 | 63,420 | 56,555 | 57,730 | 47,000 | 47,000 | 17.0 |

## TABLE 7: FILLED POSITIONS; AVERAGE, MEDIAN, AND BEGINNING SALARIES; AND AVERAGE YEARS OF EXPERIENCE IN ARL UNIVERSITY LIBRARIES, FY 2010–2011

| Institution | FILLED POSITIONS FY 2011 | AVERAGE SALARIES FY 2010 | AVERAGE SALARIES FY 2011 | MEDIAN SALARIES FY 2010 | MEDIAN SALARIES FY 2011 | BEGINNING SALARIES FY 2010 | BEGINNING SALARIES FY 2011 | AVERAGE YRS. EXP. FY 2011 |
|---|---|---|---|---|---|---|---|---|
| Illinois, Urbana ‡ | 127 | 66,755 | 69,964 | 61,645 | 65,129 | 46,000 | 50,000 | 16.2 |
| Indiana ‡ | 78 | 63,870 | 63,918 | 59,331 | 59,331 | 40,400 | 40,400 | 19.5 |
| Iowa ‡ | 65 | 62,529 | 64,501 | 55,573 | 57,840 | 41,000 | 41,000 | 18.8 |
| Iowa State ‡ | 49 | 63,217 | 65,451 | 61,664 | 63,105 | 43,000 | 44,000 | 20.5 |
| Johns Hopkins ‡ | 83 | 68,926 | 69,299 | 65,690 | 65,353 | 50,026 | 51,027 | 16.7 |
| Kansas ‡ | 85 | 60,877 | 62,232 | 54,806 | 57,417 | 51,000 | 43,000 | 16.1 |
| Kent State ‡ | 63 | 63,997 | 66,624 | 60,301 | 64,520 | 55,367 | 57,078 | 16.8 |
| Kentucky ‡ | 64 | 60,966 | 60,762 | 59,839 | 59,984 | 41,000 | 41,000 | 21.7 |
| Laval †‡ | 65 | 61,963 | 67,439 | 62,474 | 69,944 | 42,468 | 46,937 | 13.1 |
| Louisiana State | 49 | 50,821 | 51,100 | 46,462 | 46,901 | 38,000 | 38,000 | 15.1 |
| Louisville ‡ | 31 | 59,483 | 59,638 | 55,884 | 53,031 | 37,000 | 37,000 | 17.3 |
| McGill †‡ | 64 | 63,797 | 71,450 | 57,834 | 64,865 | 42,856 | 47,366 | 15.7 |
| McMaster †‡ | 45 | 61,608 | 69,041 | 62,508 | 62,118 | 40,128 | 45,945 | 17.6 |
| Manitoba †‡ | 40 | 81,855 | 91,679 | 85,771 | 95,343 | 41,845 | 46,249 | 22.9 |
| Maryland | 72 | 68,874 | 69,981 | 66,603 | 69,035 | 40,000 | 40,000 | 21.6 |
| Massachusetts ‡ | 57 | 69,882 | 72,957 | 72,263 | 73,553 | 42,155 | 42,155 | 17.4 |
| MIT ‡ | 93 | 74,430 | 77,065 | 70,959 | 73,326 | 51,750 | 52,000 | 16.6 |
| Miami ‡ | 52 | 68,278 | 69,503 | 61,728 | 65,000 | 45,000 | 45,000 | 15.6 |
| Michigan ‡ | 169 | 67,767 | 71,354 | 63,717 | 65,884 | 42,000 | 42,000 | 17.4 |
| Michigan State ‡ | 65 | 68,894 | 70,979 | 65,850 | 67,373 | 47,000 | 47,500 | 17.6 |
| Minnesota | 107 | 66,794 | 68,210 | 63,557 | 65,785 | 42,000 | 43,000 | 16.9 |
| Missouri ‡ | 36 | 59,914 | 59,710 | 55,964 | 57,127 | 40,000 | 40,000 | 21.0 |
| Montreal †‡ | 89 | 62,740 | 70,501 | 59,349 | 65,596 | 36,968 | 43,497 | 15.3 |
| Nebraska ‡ | 46 | 65,057 | 64,928 | 57,472 | 57,453 | 50,000 | 50,000 | 20.0 |
| New Mexico ‡ | 44 | 72,938 | 71,159 | 68,853 | 67,913 | 40,000 | 40,000 | 19.5 |
| New York University ‡ | 84 | 79,018 | 78,859 | 69,989 | 71,616 | 52,000 | 55,000 | 15.8 |
| North Carolina | 96 | 67,637 | 65,091 | 63,712 | 62,300 | 44,000 | 44,000 | 17.3 |
| North Carolina State ‡ | 91 | 73,019 | 72,411 | 65,000 | 65,000 | 50,000 | 52,000 | 11.1 |
| Northwestern ‡ | 89 | 67,873 | 68,146 | 63,429 | 62,995 | 43,000 | 44,000 | 16.3 |
| Notre Dame ‡ | 58 | 69,492 | 71,751 | 66,508 | 67,915 | 41,200 | 44,000 | 19.5 |
| Ohio University ‡ | 45 | 55,522 | 55,590 | 48,787 | 49,275 | 41,000 | 41,500 | 13.6 |
| Ohio State ‡ | 124 | 59,476 | 57,846 | 54,450 | 53,292 | 46,000 | 46,000 | 14.2 |
| Oklahoma | 42 | 55,853 | 55,299 | 53,742 | 53,477 | 42,000 | 42,000 | 14.6 |
| Oklahoma State ‡ | 64 | 56,580 | 56,678 | 52,657 | 51,865 | 38,000 | 38,000 | 17.5 |
| Oregon ‡ | 54 | 59,782 | 61,130 | 55,973 | 57,839 | 40,000 | 40,000 | 17.3 |
| Ottawa†‡* | 34 | N/A | 87,360 | N/A | 85,122 | N/A | 47,538 | 18.9 |
| Pennsylvania ‡ | 104 | 65,997 | 66,632 | 61,850 | 63,148 | 43,500 | 41,000 | 15.6 |
| Pennsylvania State ‡ | 143 | 67,897 | 69,465 | 64,224 | 66,258 | 42,436 | 43,709 | 19.1 |
| Pittsburgh ‡ | 65 | 66,551 | 69,211 | 60,711 | 62,897 | 34,000 | 34,000 | 19.8 |
| Princeton ‡ | 112 | 79,015 | 82,454 | 73,799 | 76,100 | 63,200 | 63,200 | 20.9 |
| Purdue ‡ | 63 | 65,573 | 65,562 | 60,513 | 61,006 | 47,000 | 47,000 | 19.3 |
| Queen's † | 32 | 80,504 | 96,157 | 83,438 | 99,005 | 44,227 | 50,446 | 21.3 |

## TABLE 7: FILLED POSITIONS; AVERAGE, MEDIAN, AND BEGINNING SALARIES; AND AVERAGE YEARS OF EXPERIENCE IN ARL UNIVERSITY LIBRARIES, FY 2010–2011

| Institution | FILLED POSITIONS FY 2011 | AVERAGE SALARIES FY 2010 | AVERAGE SALARIES FY 2011 | MEDIAN SALARIES FY 2010 | MEDIAN SALARIES FY 2011 | BEGINNING SALARIES FY 2010 | BEGINNING SALARIES FY 2011 | AVERAGE YRS. EXP. FY 2011 |
|---|---|---|---|---|---|---|---|---|
| Rice | 59 | 62,215 | 65,202 | 55,833 | 60,300 | 37,200 | 38,700 | 15.4 |
| Rochester ‡ | 67 | 55,837 | 59,814 | 53,000 | 56,059 | 38,168 | 38,983 | 16.4 |
| Rutgers ‡ | 86 | 89,058 | 91,176 | 91,751 | 91,751 | 49,286 | 50,765 | 22.5 |
| Saskatchewan † ‡ | 46 | 76,307 | 85,160 | 78,850 | 81,582 | 45,197 | 52,202 | 16.0 |
| South Carolina ‡ | 48 | 53,658 | 52,032 | 49,838 | 48,627 | 34,000 | 38,000 | 16.9 |
| Southern California ‡ | 105 | 74,479 | 76,057 | 67,650 | 69,761 | 48,500 | 48,500 | 19.6 |
| Southern Illinois | 36 | 58,264 | 59,157 | 52,536 | 56,912 | 44,000 | 44,000 | 14.9 |
| SUNY Albany ‡ | 62 | 60,964 | 64,024 | 58,822 | 62,729 | 39,000 | 39,350 | 17.3 |
| SUNY Buffalo ‡ | 72 | 72,916 | 75,265 | 69,048 | 70,554 | 45,000 | 47,000 | 19.9 |
| SUNY Stony Brook ‡ | 24 | 79,837 | 87,447 | 75,457 | 79,599 | 42,000 | 43,000 | 22.3 |
| Syracuse ‡ | 54 | 65,847 | 67,893 | 60,648 | 61,390 | None | 38,000 | 19.3 |
| Temple ‡ | 39 | 66,849 | 69,082 | 58,140 | 60,048 | 44,044 | 44,004 | 19.7 |
| Tennessee ‡ | 40 | 69,380 | 68,677 | 66,307 | 67,268 | 44,000 | 44,000 | 18.9 |
| Texas ‡ | 121 | 66,882 | 66,964 | 59,260 | 59,304 | 46,000 | 45,000 | 17.1 |
| Texas A&M ‡ | 113 | 62,441 | 64,966 | 55,704 | 59,055 | 47,500 | 48,500 | 15.0 |
| Texas Tech ‡ | 68 | 60,690 | 58,352 | 57,135 | 54,163 | 45,000 | 45,000 | 12.6 |
| Toronto † | 141 | 78,211 | 85,574 | 75,194 | 82,254 | 44,484 | 49,451 | 15.6 |
| Tulane | 35 | 60,534 | 62,835 | 56,325 | 59,492 | 40,000 | 40,000 | 17.9 |
| Utah | 58 | 61,470 | 61,061 | 56,312 | 55,375 | 44,000 | 45,000 | 19.2 |
| Vanderbilt ‡ | 62 | 58,991 | 59,927 | 54,655 | 55,945 | 40,500 | 41,000 | 18.0 |
| Virginia ‡ | 72 | 67,988 | 70,351 | 60,000 | 64,600 | 44,000 | 44,000 | 17.7 |
| Virginia Tech ‡ | 38 | 63,148 | 63,308 | 58,540 | 58,540 | 40,000 | 40,000 | 16.8 |
| Washington ‡ | 115 | 66,476 | 65,466 | 59,934 | 58,752 | 42,600 | 42,600 | 19.2 |
| Washington State ‡ | 42 | 62,755 | 63,512 | 58,172 | 58,172 | 38,500 | 38,500 | 19.6 |
| Washington U.-St. Louis ‡ | 62 | 59,037 | 60,832 | 53,740 | 55,489 | 40,000 | 40,000 | 17.2 |
| Waterloo † ‡ | 36 | 70,230 | 76,645 | 70,260 | 75,974 | 44,402 | 49,110 | 17.4 |
| Wayne State ‡ | 73 | 61,261 | 60,697 | 54,705 | 55,396 | 40,500 | 41,000 | 13.4 |
| Western Ontario † ‡ | 65 | 59,073 | 68,581 | 55,725 | 66,961 | 40,610 | 47,836 | 13.4 |
| Wisconsin ‡ | 155 | 61,856 | 61,068 | 58,654 | 57,692 | 40,526 | 40,526 | 18.1 |
| Yale ‡ | 191 | 81,088 | 80,642 | 76,300 | 76,365 | 50,500 | 50,500 | 19.0 |
| York † ‡ | 53 | 82,297 | 99,770 | 77,321 | 96,446 | 41,999 | 46,419 | 17.6 |

Excludes medical and law libraries. See Tables 35 and 42 for comparable figures for medical and law libraries.

Directors are included in figures for average years of experience and filled positions, but not in either the average or median salary statistics.

† Canadian salaries are expressed in US dollars.

‡ See Footnotes.

* Ottawa became a member in 2010 and was included for the first time in the *ARL Annual Salary Survey 2010–2011*.

PAGE INTENTIONALLY LEFT BLANK.

## TABLE 8: BEGINNING PROFESSIONAL SALARIES IN ARL UNIVERSITY LIBRARIES
## RANK ORDER TABLE, FY 2009–2010

| Rank | Institution | Salary | Rank | Institution | Salary |
|---|---|---|---|---|---|
| 1 | Princeton | 63,200 | 58 | Delaware | 43,600 |
| 2 | Kent State | 55,367 | 59 | Pennsylvania | 43,500 |
| 3 | New York | 52,000 | 60 | Alberta | 43,398 |
| 4 | MIT | 51,750 | 61 | Arizona State | 43,000 |
| 5 | Columbia | 51,500 | 61 | Houston | 43,000 |
| 6 | Guelph | 51,169 | 61 | Iowa State | 43,000 |
| 7 | Brigham Young | 51,000 | 61 | Northwestern | 43,000 |
| 7 | Kansas | 51,000 | 65 | McGill | 42,856 |
| 9 | Yale | 50,500 | 66 | Hawaii | 42,660 |
| 10 | Johns Hopkins | 50,026 | 67 | Washington | 42,600 |
| 11 | Nebraska | 50,000 | 68 | Laval | 42,468 |
| 11 | North Carolina State | 50,000 | 69 | Pennsylvania State | 42,436 |
| 13 | Calgary | 49,713 | 70 | Boston College | 42,300 |
| 14 | Rutgers | 49,286 | 71 | Massachusetts | 42,155 |
| 15 | Harvard | 48,800 | 72 | Alabama | 42,000 |
| 16 | Arizona | 48,605 | 72 | Emory | 42,000 |
| 17 | Southern California | 48,500 | 72 | Florida | 42,000 |
| 18 | Chicago | 48,204 | 72 | Florida State | 42,000 |
| 19 | Connecticut | 48,000 | 72 | Michigan | 42,000 |
| 20 | Texas A&M | 47,500 | 72 | Minnesota | 42,000 |
| 21 | British Columbia | 47,429 | 72 | Oklahoma | 42,000 |
| 22 | Calif. Berkeley | 47,087 | 72 | SUNY Stony Brook | 42,000 |
| 22 | Calif. Riverside | 47,087 | 80 | York | 41,999 |
| 24 | Cornell | 47,000 | 81 | Manitoba | 41,845 |
| 24 | George Washington | 47,000 | 82 | Notre Dame | 41,200 |
| 24 | Illinois, Chicago | 47,000 | 83 | Iowa | 41,000 |
| 24 | Michigan State | 47,000 | 83 | Kentucky | 41,000 |
| 24 | Purdue | 47,000 | 83 | Ohio | 41,000 |
| 29 | Calif. Davis | 46,164 | 86 | Western Ontario | 40,610 |
| 29 | Calif. Irvine | 46,164 | 87 | Wisconsin | 40,526 |
| 29 | Calif. Los Angeles | 46,164 | 88 | Vanderbilt | 40,500 |
| 29 | Calif. San Diego | 46,164 | 88 | Wayne State | 40,500 |
| 29 | Calif. Santa Barbara | 46,164 | 90 | Indiana | 40,400 |
| 34 | Illinois, Urbana | 46,000 | 91 | McMaster | 40,128 |
| 34 | Ohio State | 46,000 | 92 | Cincinnati | 40,000 |
| 34 | Texas | 46,000 | 92 | Maryland | 40,000 |
| 37 | Dartmouth | 45,500 | 92 | Missouri | 40,000 |
| 38 | Saskatchewan | 45,197 | 92 | New Mexico | 40,000 |
| 39 | Colorado State | 45,000 | 92 | Oregon | 40,000 |
| 39 | Duke | 45,000 | 92 | Tulane | 40,000 |
| 39 | Georgetown | 45,000 | 92 | Virginia Tech | 40,000 |
| 39 | Miami | 45,000 | 92 | Washington-St. Louis | 40,000 |
| 39 | SUNY Buffalo | 45,000 | 100 | Brown | 39,500 |
| 39 | Texas Tech | 45,000 | 101 | SUNY Albany | 39,000 |
| 45 | Auburn | 44,720 | 102 | Washington State | 38,500 |
| 46 | Toronto | 44,484 | 103 | Rochester | 38,168 |
| 47 | Waterloo | 44,402 | 104 | Georgia | 38,000 |
| 48 | Queen's | 44,227 | 104 | Howard | 38,000 |
| 49 | Temple | 44,044 | 104 | Louisiana State | 38,000 |
| 50 | Colorado | 44,000 | 104 | Oklahoma State | 38,000 |
| 50 | Georgia Tech | 44,000 | 108 | Rice | 37,200 |
| 50 | North Carolina | 44,000 | 109 | Louisville | 37,000 |
| 50 | Southern Illinois | 44,000 | 110 | Montreal | 36,968 |
| 50 | Tennessee | 44,000 | 111 | Case Western Reserve | 35,000 |
| 50 | Utah | 44,000 | 112 | Pittsburgh | 34,000 |
| 50 | Virginia | 44,000 | 112 | South Carolina | 34,000 |
| 57 | Boston University | 43,700 | N/A | Syracuse | None |

Reprinted from *ARL Annual Salary Survey 2009–2010*. Beginning salary figures represent officially designated base, not necessarily salaries of actual incumbents.

Excludes medical and law libraries. See Tables 36 and 43 for comparable figures for medical and law libraries.

Canadian salaries are expressed in US dollars.

# TABLE 9: BEGINNING PROFESSIONAL SALARIES IN ARL UNIVERSITY LIBRARIES

## RANK ORDER TABLE, FY 2010–2011

| Rank | Institution | Salary | Rank | Institution | Salary |
|---|---|---|---|---|---|
| 1 | Princeton | 63,200 | 59 | Colorado | 44,000 |
| 2 | Guelph | 58,392 | 59 | Georgia Tech | 44,000 |
| 3 | Kent State | 57,078 | 59 | Houston | 44,000 |
| 4 | Colorado State | 55,000 | 59 | Iowa State | 44,000 |
| 4 | New York University | 55,000 | 59 | North Carolina | 44,000 |
| 6 | Calgary | 54,945 | 59 | Northwestern | 44,000 |
| 7 | Harvard | 53,093 | 59 | Notre Dame | 44,000 |
| 8 | Alberta | 52,833 | 59 | Southern Illinois | 44,000 |
| 9 | British Columbia | 52,420 | 59 | Tennessee | 44,000 |
| 10 | Saskatchewan | 52,202 | 59 | Virginia | 44,000 |
| 11 | Brigham Young | 52,020 | 69 | Pennsylvania State | 43,709 |
| 12 | Columbia | 52,000 | 70 | Delaware | 43,600 |
| 12 | MIT | 52,000 | 71 | Montreal | 43,497 |
| 12 | North Carolina State | 52,000 | 72 | Boston College | 43,350 |
| 15 | Johns Hopkins | 51,027 | 73 | Arizona State | 43,000 |
| 16 | Arizona | 50,857 | 73 | Kansas | 43,000 |
| 17 | Rutgers | 50,765 | 73 | Minnesota | 43,000 |
| 18 | Yale | 50,500 | 73 | SUNY Stony Brook | 43,000 |
| 19 | Queen's | 50,446 | 77 | Washington | 42,600 |
| 20 | Chicago | 50,151 | 78 | Massachusetts | 42,155 |
| 21 | Connecticut | 50,000 | 79 | Alabama | 42,000 |
| 21 | Illinois, Urbana | 50,000 | 79 | Cincinnati | 42,000 |
| 21 | Nebraska | 50,000 | 79 | Florida | 42,000 |
| 24 | Toronto | 49,451 | 79 | Florida State | 42,000 |
| 25 | Waterloo | 49,110 | 79 | Michigan | 42,000 |
| 26 | Southern California | 48,500 | 79 | Oklahoma | 42,000 |
| 26 | Texas A&M | 48,500 | 85 | Ohio University | 41,500 |
| 28 | Cornell | 48,000 | 86 | Iowa | 41,000 |
| 29 | Western Ontario | 47,836 | 86 | Kentucky | 41,000 |
| 30 | Emory | 47,750 | 86 | Pennsylvania | 41,000 |
| 31 | Ottawa | 47,538 | 86 | Vanderbilt | 41,000 |
| 32 | Michigan State | 47,500 | 86 | Wayne State | 41,000 |
| 33 | McGill | 47,366 | 91 | Wisconsin | 40,526 |
| 34 | California, Riverside | 47,087 | 92 | Brown | 40,500 |
| 35 | George Washington | 47,000 | 93 | Indiana | 40,400 |
| 35 | Illinois, Chicago | 47,000 | 94 | Maryland | 40,000 |
| 35 | Purdue | 47,000 | 94 | Missouri | 40,000 |
| 35 | SUNY Buffalo | 47,000 | 94 | New Mexico | 40,000 |
| 39 | Laval | 46,937 | 94 | Oregon | 40,000 |
| 40 | York | 46,419 | 94 | Tulane | 40,000 |
| 41 | Manitoba | 46,249 | 94 | Virginia Tech | 40,000 |
| 42 | California, Berkeley | 46,164 | 94 | Washington U.-St. Louis | 40,000 |
| 42 | California, Davis | 46,164 | 101 | SUNY Albany | 39,350 |
| 42 | California, Los Angeles | 46,164 | 102 | Rochester | 38,983 |
| 42 | California, San Diego | 46,164 | 103 | Rice | 38,700 |
| 42 | California, Santa Barbara | 46,164 | 104 | Washington State | 38,500 |
| 47 | California, Irvine | 46,144 | 105 | Georgia | 38,000 |
| 48 | Ohio State | 46,000 | 105 | Louisiana State | 38,000 |
| 49 | McMaster | 45,945 | 105 | Oklahoma State | 38,000 |
| 50 | Dartmouth | 45,500 | 105 | South Carolina | 38,000 |
| 51 | Duke | 45,000 | 105 | Syracuse | 38,000 |
| 51 | Georgetown | 45,000 | 110 | Louisville | 37,000 |
| 51 | Miami | 45,000 | 111 | Case Western Reserve | 35,000 |
| 51 | Texas | 45,000 | 111 | Hawaii | 35,000 |
| 51 | Texas Tech | 45,000 | 113 | Howard | 34,627 |
| 51 | Utah | 45,000 | 114 | Pittsburgh | 34,000 |
| 57 | Auburn | 44,720 | 115 | Boston University | 33,000 |
| 58 | Temple | 44,004 | | | |

Beginning salary figures represent officially designated base, not necessarily salaries of actual incumbents.
Excludes medical and law libraries. See Tables 36 and 43 for comparable figures for medical and law libraries.
Canadian salaries are expressed in US dollars.

# TABLE 10: MEDIAN PROFESSIONAL SALARIES IN ARL UNIVERSITY LIBRARIES
## RANK ORDER TABLE, FY 2009–2010

| Rank | Institution | Salary | Rank | Institution | Salary |
|---|---|---|---|---|---|
| 1 | Rutgers | 91,751 | 58 | Pennsylvania | 61,850 |
| 2 | Alberta | 89,319 | 59 | Miami | 61,728 |
| 3 | California, Davis | 88,488 | 60 | Iowa State | 61,664 |
| 4 | Manitoba | 85,771 | 61 | Illinois, Urbana | 61,645 |
| 5 | Queen's | 83,438 | 62 | Brown | 61,549 |
| 6 | California, Berkeley | 82,524 | 63 | Pittsburgh | 60,711 |
| 7 | Saskatchewan | 78,850 | 64 | Syracuse | 60,648 |
| 8 | Connecticut | 78,079 | 65 | Purdue | 60,513 |
| 9 | York | 77,321 | 66 | Kent State | 60,301 |
| 10 | Calgary | 76,749 | 67 | Duke | 60,000 |
| | | | | | |
| 11 | Yale | 76,300 | 67 | Virginia | 60,000 |
| 12 | California, Irvine | 75,708 | 69 | Washington | 59,934 |
| 12 | California, Los Angeles | 75,708 | 70 | Arizona | 59,915 |
| 12 | California, Riverside | 75,708 | 71 | Kentucky | 59,839 |
| 12 | California, San Diego | 75,708 | 72 | Montreal | 59,349 |
| 16 | SUNY Stony Brook | 75,457 | 73 | Indiana | 59,331 |
| 17 | Toronto | 75,194 | 74 | Texas | 59,260 |
| 18 | Princeton | 73,799 | 75 | SUNY Albany | 58,822 |
| 19 | Delaware | 73,353 | 76 | Wisconsin | 58,654 |
| 20 | Chicago | 72,329 | 77 | Virginia Tech | 58,540 |
| | | | | | |
| 21 | Massachusetts | 72,263 | 78 | Washington State | 58,172 |
| 22 | MIT | 70,959 | 79 | Temple | 58,140 |
| 23 | Harvard | 70,720 | 80 | Georgia Tech | 58,016 |
| 24 | Waterloo | 70,260 | 81 | McGill | 57,834 |
| 25 | British Columbia | 70,005 | 82 | Nebraska | 57,472 |
| 26 | New York University | 69,989 | 83 | Texas Tech | 57,135 |
| 27 | SUNY Buffalo | 69,048 | 84 | Boston University | 56,600 |
| 28 | California, Santa Barbara | 68,892 | 85 | Houston | 56,563 |
| 29 | New Mexico | 68,853 | 86 | Illinois, Chicago | 56,555 |
| 30 | Dartmouth | 67,933 | 87 | Florida | 56,388 |
| | | | | | |
| 31 | Southern California | 67,650 | 88 | Tulane | 56,325 |
| 32 | Boston College | 67,280 | 89 | Utah | 56,312 |
| 33 | George Washington | 67,143 | 90 | Oregon | 55,973 |
| 34 | Guelph | 66,902 | 91 | Missouri | 55,964 |
| 35 | Maryland | 66,603 | 92 | Louisville | 55,884 |
| 36 | Notre Dame | 66,508 | 93 | Rice | 55,833 |
| 37 | Tennessee | 66,307 | 94 | Western Ontario | 55,725 |
| 38 | Hawaii | 66,225 | 95 | Texas A&M | 55,704 |
| 39 | Michigan State | 65,850 | 96 | Iowa | 55,573 |
| 40 | Johns Hopkins | 65,690 | 97 | Case Western Reserve | 55,227 |
| | | | | | |
| 41 | Colorado State | 65,300 | 98 | Kansas | 54,806 |
| 42 | Arizona State | 65,071 | 99 | Wayne State | 54,705 |
| 43 | North Carolina State | 65,000 | 100 | Vanderbilt | 54,655 |
| 44 | Colorado | 64,573 | 101 | Ohio State | 54,450 |
| 45 | Columbia | 64,385 | 102 | Oklahoma | 53,742 |
| 46 | Cornell | 64,239 | 103 | Washington U.-St. Louis | 53,740 |
| 47 | Pennsylvania State | 64,224 | 104 | Auburn | 53,705 |
| 48 | Brigham Young | 63,950 | 105 | Rochester | 53,000 |
| 49 | Michigan | 63,717 | 106 | Oklahoma State | 52,657 |
| 50 | North Carolina | 63,712 | 107 | Southern Illinois | 52,536 |
| | | | | | |
| 51 | Minnesota | 63,557 | 108 | Alabama | 52,204 |
| 52 | Georgetown | 63,538 | 109 | Georgia | 50,000 |
| 53 | Northwestern | 63,429 | 110 | South Carolina | 49,838 |
| 54 | Emory | 63,068 | 111 | Florida State | 49,805 |
| 55 | McMaster | 62,508 | 112 | Ohio University | 48,787 |
| 56 | Laval | 62,474 | 113 | Louisiana State | 46,462 |
| 57 | Cincinnati | 61,879 | 114 | Howard | 43,010 |

Reprinted from *ARL Annual Salary Survey 2009–2010*. Salaries of directors are not included in the calculation of medians.
Excludes medical and law libraries. See Tables 37 and 44 for comparable figures for medical and law libraries.
Canadian salaries are expressed in US dollars.

## TABLE 11: MEDIAN PROFESSIONAL SALARIES IN ARL UNIVERSITY LIBRARIES

## RANK ORDER TABLE, FY 2010–2011

| Rank | Institution | Salary | Rank | Institution | Salary |
|---|---|---|---|---|---|
| 1 | Queen's | 99,005 | 59 | Kent State | 64,520 |
| 2 | Alberta | 96,759 | 60 | Georgetown | 63,965 |
| 3 | York | 96,446 | 61 | Emory | 63,198 |
| 4 | Manitoba | 95,343 | 62 | Pennsylvania | 63,148 |
| 5 | Rutgers | 91,751 | 63 | Iowa State | 63,105 |
| 6 | Calgary | 88,732 | 64 | Northwestern | 62,995 |
| 7 | California, Davis | 88,488 | 65 | Brown | 62,972 |
| 8 | Ottawa | 85,122 | 66 | Pittsburgh | 62,897 |
| 9 | British Columbia | 83,131 | 67 | SUNY Albany | 62,729 |
| 10 | California, Berkeley | 82,524 | 68 | North Carolina | 62,300 |
| 11 | Toronto | 82,254 | 69 | McMaster | 62,118 |
| 12 | Saskatchewan | 81,582 | 70 | Syracuse | 61,390 |
| 13 | SUNY Stony Brook | 79,599 | 71 | Colorado | 61,262 |
| 14 | Connecticut | 79,309 | 72 | Purdue | 61,006 |
| 15 | California, Riverside | 79,116 | 73 | Rice | 60,300 |
| 16 | Guelph | 76,872 | 74 | Temple | 60,048 |
| 17 | Yale | 76,365 | 75 | Duke | 60,000 |
| 18 | Princeton | 76,100 | 76 | Kentucky | 59,984 |
| 19 | Waterloo | 75,974 | 77 | Tulane | 59,492 |
| 20 | California, Irvine | 75,708 | 78 | Indiana | 59,331 |
| 20 | California, Los Angeles | 75,708 | 79 | Texas | 59,304 |
| 20 | California, San Diego | 75,708 | 80 | Arizona | 59,118 |
| 23 | California, Santa Barbara | 74,104 | 81 | Texas A&M | 59,055 |
| 24 | Massachusetts | 73,553 | 82 | Washington | 58,752 |
| 25 | MIT | 73,326 | 83 | Virginia Tech | 58,540 |
| 26 | Chicago | 73,130 | 84 | Washington State | 58,172 |
| 27 | Delaware | 72,868 | 85 | Florida | 58,073 |
| 28 | George Washington | 72,277 | 86 | Georgia Tech | 58,016 |
| 29 | Harvard | 72,134 | 87 | Iowa | 57,840 |
| 30 | New York University | 71,616 | 88 | Oregon | 57,839 |
| 31 | SUNY Buffalo | 70,554 | 89 | Illinois, Chicago | 57,730 |
| 32 | Laval | 69,944 | 90 | Wisconsin | 57,692 |
| 33 | Southern California | 69,761 | 91 | Nebraska | 57,453 |
| 34 | Boston College | 69,560 | 92 | Kansas | 57,417 |
| 35 | Maryland | 69,035 | 93 | Boston University | 57,200 |
| 36 | Notre Dame | 67,915 | 94 | Missouri | 57,127 |
| 37 | New Mexico | 67,913 | 95 | Southern Illinois | 56,912 |
| 38 | Michigan State | 67,373 | 96 | Rochester | 56,059 |
| 39 | Tennessee | 67,268 | 97 | Vanderbilt | 55,945 |
| 40 | Dartmouth | 67,159 | 98 | Washington U.-St. Louis | 55,489 |
| 41 | Western Ontario | 66,961 | 99 | Case Western Reserve | 55,434 |
| 42 | Cornell | 66,873 | 100 | Wayne State | 55,396 |
| 43 | Cincinnati | 66,260 | 101 | Utah | 55,375 |
| 44 | Pennsylvania State | 66,258 | 102 | Alabama | 55,188 |
| 45 | Brigham Young | 66,000 | 103 | Houston | 54,628 |
| 46 | Michigan | 65,884 | 104 | Texas Tech | 54,163 |
| 47 | Minnesota | 65,785 | 105 | Oklahoma | 53,477 |
| 48 | Montreal | 65,596 | 106 | Ohio State | 53,292 |
| 49 | Johns Hopkins | 65,353 | 107 | Louisville | 53,031 |
| 50 | Columbia | 65,280 | 108 | Auburn | 52,330 |
| 51 | Illinois, Urbana | 65,129 | 109 | Florida State | 52,265 |
| 52 | Arizona State | 65,039 | 110 | Oklahoma State | 51,865 |
| 53 | Miami | 65,000 | 111 | Howard | 50,223 |
| 53 | North Carolina State | 65,000 | 112 | Georgia | 49,795 |
| 55 | McGill | 64,865 | 113 | Ohio University | 49,275 |
| 56 | Colorado State | 64,700 | 114 | South Carolina | 48,627 |
| 57 | Hawaii | 64,692 | 115 | Louisiana State | 46,901 |
| 58 | Virginia | 64,600 | | | |

Salaries of directors are not included in the calculation of medians.

Excludes medical and law libraries. See Tables 37 and 44 for comparable figures for medical and law libraries.

Canadian salaries are expressed in US dollars.

## Table 12: Average Professional Salaries in ARL University Libraries
## Rank Order Table, FY 2009–2010

| Rank | Institution | Salary | Rank | Institution | Salary |
|---|---|---|---|---|---|
| 1 | Rutgers | 89,058 | 58 | Pittsburgh | 66,551 |
| 2 | Alberta | 84,172 | 59 | Washington | 66,476 |
| 3 | California, Berkeley | 83,853 | 60 | Arizona State | 66,091 |
| 4 | York | 82,297 | 61 | Brigham Young | 66,005 |
| 5 | Connecticut | 82,083 | 62 | Pennsylvania | 65,997 |
| 6 | Manitoba | 81,855 | 63 | Arizona | 65,897 |
| 7 | Calgary | 81,275 | 64 | Brown | 65,880 |
| 8 | California, Davis | 81,135 | 65 | Syracuse | 65,847 |
| 9 | Yale | 81,088 | 66 | Purdue | 65,573 |
| 10 | Queen's | 80,504 | 67 | Cincinnati | 65,445 |
| 11 | SUNY Stony Brook | 79,837 | 68 | Nebraska | 65,057 |
| 12 | New York University | 79,018 | 69 | Duke | 64,870 |
| 13 | Princeton | 79,015 | 70 | Kent State | 63,997 |
| 14 | Toronto | 78,211 | 71 | Indiana | 63,870 |
| 15 | California, Los Angeles | 78,189 | 72 | McGill | 63,797 |
| 16 | California, Riverside | 77,661 | 73 | Georgia Tech | 63,526 |
| 17 | Harvard | 77,319 | 74 | Iowa State | 63,217 |
| 18 | California, San Diego | 77,158 | 75 | Virginia Tech | 63,148 |
| 19 | California, Irvine | 76,645 | 76 | Washington State | 62,755 |
| 20 | Saskatchewan | 76,307 | 77 | Montreal | 62,740 |
| 21 | Chicago | 76,254 | 78 | Iowa | 62,529 |
| 22 | Delaware | 75,703 | 79 | Texas A&M | 62,441 |
| 23 | Southern California | 74,479 | 80 | Rice | 62,215 |
| 24 | MIT | 74,430 | 81 | Illinois, Chicago | 62,208 |
| 25 | George Washington | 74,353 | 82 | Laval | 61,963 |
| 26 | British Columbia | 73,023 | 83 | Wisconsin | 61,856 |
| 27 | North Carolina State | 73,019 | 84 | Houston | 61,669 |
| 28 | Columbia | 72,939 | 85 | McMaster | 61,608 |
| 29 | New Mexico | 72,938 | 86 | Utah | 61,470 |
| 30 | SUNY Buffalo | 72,916 | 87 | Wayne State | 61,261 |
| 31 | Dartmouth | 72,208 | 88 | Kentucky | 60,966 |
| 32 | Cornell | 71,548 | 89 | SUNY Albany | 60,964 |
| 33 | California, Santa Barbara | 71,378 | 90 | Kansas | 60,877 |
| 34 | Waterloo | 70,230 | 91 | Texas Tech | 60,690 |
| 35 | Massachusetts | 69,882 | 92 | Tulane | 60,534 |
| 36 | Boston College | 69,739 | 93 | Florida | 60,450 |
| 37 | Notre Dame | 69,492 | 94 | Missouri | 59,914 |
| 38 | Tennessee | 69,380 | 95 | Oregon | 59,782 |
| 39 | Georgetown | 69,227 | 96 | Louisville | 59,483 |
| 40 | Guelph | 69,113 | 97 | Ohio State | 59,476 |
| 41 | Johns Hopkins | 68,926 | 98 | Western Ontario | 59,073 |
| 42 | Michigan State | 68,894 | 99 | Washington U.-St. Louis | 59,037 |
| 43 | Maryland | 68,874 | 100 | Vanderbilt | 58,991 |
| 44 | Emory | 68,747 | 101 | Case Western Reserve | 58,788 |
| 45 | Colorado State | 68,311 | 102 | Auburn | 58,382 |
| 46 | Miami | 68,278 | 103 | Alabama | 58,272 |
| 47 | Virginia | 67,988 | 104 | Southern Illinois | 58,264 |
| 48 | Pennsylvania State | 67,897 | 105 | Boston University | 57,615 |
| 49 | Northwestern | 67,873 | 106 | Oklahoma State | 56,580 |
| 50 | Michigan | 67,767 | 107 | Georgia | 56,544 |
| 51 | North Carolina | 67,637 | 108 | Oklahoma | 55,853 |
| 52 | Colorado | 67,523 | 109 | Rochester | 55,837 |
| 53 | Texas | 66,882 | 110 | Ohio University | 55,522 |
| 54 | Temple | 66,849 | 111 | Florida State | 54,858 |
| 55 | Minnesota | 66,794 | 112 | South Carolina | 53,658 |
| 56 | Illinois, Urbana | 66,755 | 113 | Louisiana State | 50,821 |
| 57 | Hawaii | 66,721 | 114 | Howard | 43,547 |

Reprinted from *ARL Annual Salary Survey 2009–2010*. Salaries of directors are not included in the calculation of averages.

Excludes medical and law libraries. See Tables 38 and 45 for comparable figures for medical and law libraries.

Canadian salaries are expressed in US dollars.

## TABLE 13: Average Professional Salaries in ARL University Libraries

## Rank Order Table, FY 2010–2011

| Rank | Institution | Salary | Rank | Institution | Salary |
|------|-------------|--------|------|-------------|--------|
| 1 | York | 99,770 | 59 | Northwestern | 68,146 |
| 2 | Alberta | 96,215 | 60 | Syracuse | 67,893 |
| 3 | Queen's | 96,157 | 61 | Colorado State | 67,844 |
| 4 | Calgary | 91,776 | 62 | Laval | 67,439 |
| 5 | Manitoba | 91,679 | 63 | Brigham Young | 67,295 |
| 6 | Rutgers | 91,176 | 64 | Texas | 66,964 |
| 7 | SUNY Stony Brook | 87,447 | 65 | Pennsylvania | 66,632 |
| 8 | Ottawa | 87,360 | 66 | Kent State | 66,624 |
| 9 | Toronto | 85,574 | 67 | Brown | 66,368 |
| 10 | California, Berkeley | 85,329 | 68 | Purdue | 65,562 |
| 11 | Saskatchewan | 85,160 | 69 | Duke | 65,526 |
| 12 | British Columbia | 85,029 | 70 | Washington | 65,466 |
| 13 | California, Davis | 84,334 | 71 | Iowa State | 65,451 |
| 14 | Princeton | 82,454 | 72 | Arizona | 65,351 |
| 15 | Connecticut | 81,341 | 73 | Rice | 65,202 |
| 16 | Yale | 80,642 | 74 | North Carolina | 65,091 |
| 17 | Guelph | 80,588 | 75 | Texas A&M | 64,966 |
| 18 | California, Riverside | 79,762 | 76 | Nebraska | 64,928 |
| 19 | California, Los Angeles | 79,113 | 77 | Arizona State | 64,744 |
| 20 | Harvard | 79,111 | 78 | Colorado | 64,595 |
| 21 | New York University | 78,859 | 79 | Iowa | 64,501 |
| 22 | California, Irvine | 77,825 | 80 | SUNY Albany | 64,024 |
| 23 | MIT | 77,065 | 81 | Indiana | 63,918 |
| 24 | California, San Diego | 77,064 | 82 | Georgia Tech | 63,534 |
| 25 | George Washington | 76,999 | 83 | Washington State | 63,512 |
| 26 | Chicago | 76,692 | 84 | Illinois, Chicago | 63,420 |
| 27 | Delaware | 76,673 | 85 | Virginia Tech | 63,308 |
| 28 | Waterloo | 76,645 | 86 | Hawaii | 63,037 |
| 29 | Southern California | 76,057 | 87 | Tulane | 62,835 |
| 30 | SUNY Buffalo | 75,265 | 88 | Kansas | 62,232 |
| 31 | California, Santa Barbara | 74,431 | 89 | Florida | 62,229 |
| 32 | Cornell | 74,377 | 90 | Houston | 62,188 |
| 33 | Columbia | 74,360 | 91 | Oregon | 61,130 |
| 34 | Massachusetts | 72,957 | 92 | Wisconsin | 61,068 |
| 35 | North Carolina State | 72,411 | 93 | Utah | 61,061 |
| 36 | Notre Dame | 71,751 | 94 | Washington U.-St. Louis | 60,832 |
| 37 | McGill | 71,450 | 95 | Kentucky | 60,762 |
| 38 | Michigan | 71,354 | 96 | Wayne State | 60,697 |
| 39 | New Mexico | 71,159 | 97 | Vanderbilt | 59,927 |
| 40 | Michigan State | 70,979 | 98 | Rochester | 59,814 |
| 41 | Boston College | 70,871 | 99 | Missouri | 59,710 |
| 42 | Dartmouth | 70,594 | 100 | Boston University | 59,680 |
| 43 | Montreal | 70,501 | 101 | Louisville | 59,638 |
| 44 | Virginia | 70,351 | 102 | Southern Illinois | 59,157 |
| 45 | Georgetown | 70,338 | 103 | Case Western Reserve | 58,886 |
| 46 | Maryland | 69,981 | 104 | Alabama | 58,760 |
| 47 | Illinois, Urbana | 69,964 | 105 | Texas Tech | 58,352 |
| 48 | Emory | 69,761 | 106 | Ohio State | 57,846 |
| 49 | Miami | 69,503 | 107 | Auburn | 57,728 |
| 50 | Pennsylvania State | 69,465 | 108 | Oklahoma State | 56,678 |
| 51 | Johns Hopkins | 69,299 | 109 | Howard | 56,590 |
| 52 | Pittsburgh | 69,211 | 110 | Florida State | 56,313 |
| 53 | Temple | 69,082 | 111 | Georgia | 56,057 |
| 54 | McMaster | 69,041 | 112 | Ohio University | 55,590 |
| 55 | Tennessee | 68,677 | 113 | Oklahoma | 55,299 |
| 56 | Western Ontario | 68,581 | 114 | South Carolina | 52,032 |
| 57 | Cincinnati | 68,451 | 115 | Louisiana State | 51,100 |
| 58 | Minnesota | 68,210 | | | |

Salaries of directors are not included in the calculation of averages.

Excludes medical and law libraries. See Tables 38 and 45 for comparable figures for medical and law libraries.

Canadian salaries are expressed in US dollars.

## TABLE 14: AVERAGE, MEDIAN, AND BEGINNING PROFESSIONAL SALARIES IN ARL UNIVERSITY LIBRARIES SUMMARY OF RANKINGS, FYS 2007–2008 TO 2010–2011

| Institution | Average Salaries | | | | Median Salaries | | | | Beginning Salaries | | | |
| --- | --- | --- | --- | --- | --- | --- | --- | --- | --- | --- | --- | --- |
| FY | 2008 | 2009 | 2010 | 2011 | 2008 | 2009 | 2010 | 2011 | 2008 | 2009 | 2010 | 2011 |
| Alabama | 92 | 97 | 103 | 104 | 96 | 105 | 108 | 102 | 74 | 73 | 72 | 79 |
| Alberta | 11 | 4 | 2 | 2 | 2 | 1 | 2 | 2 | 38 | 8 | 60 | 8 |
| Arizona | 56 | 65 | 63 | 72 | 56 | 62 | 70 | 80 | 7 | 26 | 16 | 16 |
| Arizona State | 59 | 77 | 60 | 77 | 41 | 66 | 42 | 52 | 34 | 60 | 61 | 73 |
| Auburn | 75 | 90 | 102 | 107 | 63 | 90 | 104 | 108 | 25 | 50 | 45 | 57 |
| Boston University | 106 | 40 | 105 | 100 | 100 | 91 | 84 | 93 | 62 | 70 | 57 | 115 |
| Boston College | 35 | 95 | 36 | 41 | 31 | 35 | 32 | 34 | 57 | 70 | 70 | 72 |
| Brigham Young | 70 | 72 | 61 | 63 | 55 | 60 | 48 | 45 | 14 | 22 | 7 | 11 |
| British Columbia | 26 | 10 | 26 | 12 | 22 | 9 | 25 | 9 | 15 | 2 | 21 | 9 |
| Brown | 47 | 53 | 64 | 67 | 42 | 51 | 62 | 65 | 94 | 99 | 100 | 92 |
| Calgary | N/A | N/A | 7 | 4 | N/A | N/A | 10 | 6 | N/A | N/A | 13 | 6 |
| California, Berkeley | 3 | 8 | 3 | 10 | 5 | 10 | 6 | 10 | 69 | 35 | 22 | 42 |
| California, Davis | 15 | 12 | 8 | 13 | 3 | 8 | 3 | 7 | 69 | 35 | 29 | 42 |
| California, Irvine | 20 | 20 | 19 | 22 | 13 | 16 | 12 | 20 | 69 | 35 | 29 | 47 |
| California, Los Angeles | 10 | 23 | 15 | 19 | 12 | 19 | 12 | 20 | 69 | 35 | 29 | 42 |
| California, Riverside | 28 | 26 | 16 | 18 | 24 | 18 | 12 | 15 | 41 | 27 | 22 | 34 |
| California, San Diego | 14 | 21 | 18 | 24 | 13 | 16 | 12 | 20 | 69 | 35 | 29 | 42 |
| California, Santa Barbara | 23 | 32 | 33 | 31 | 27 | 31 | 28 | 23 | 43 | 35 | 29 | 42 |
| Case Western Reserve | 96 | 98 | 101 | 103 | 90 | 96 | 97 | 99 | 108 | 110 | 111 | 111 |
| Chicago | 18 | 25 | 21 | 26 | 23 | 28 | 20 | 26 | 12 | 21 | 18 | 20 |
| Cincinnati | 49 | 60 | 67 | 57 | 47 | 64 | 57 | 43 | 94 | 100 | 92 | 79 |
| Colorado | 46 | 61 | 52 | 78 | 49 | 48 | 44 | 71 | 58 | 51 | 50 | 59 |
| Colorado State | 68 | 48 | 45 | 61 | 53 | 45 | 41 | 56 | 29 | 42 | 39 | 4 |
| Columbia | 21 | 31 | 28 | 33 | 46 | 49 | 45 | 50 | 1 | 4 | 5 | 12 |
| Connecticut | 7 | 11 | 5 | 15 | 9 | 12 | 8 | 14 | 5 | 22 | 19 | 21 |
| Cornell | 33 | 41 | 32 | 32 | 40 | 55 | 46 | 42 | 16 | 28 | 24 | 28 |
| Dartmouth | 19 | 30 | 31 | 42 | 16 | 30 | 30 | 40 | 74 | 67 | 37 | 50 |
| Delaware | 29 | 29 | 22 | 27 | 34 | 24 | 19 | 27 | 28 | 58 | 58 | 70 |
| Duke | 76 | 78 | 69 | 69 | 81 | 78 | 67 | 75 | 34 | 51 | 39 | 51 |
| Emory | 57 | 46 | 44 | 48 | 51 | 54 | 54 | 61 | 94 | 83 | 72 | 30 |
| Florida | 100 | 96 | 93 | 89 | 98 | 92 | 87 | 85 | 44 | 73 | 72 | 79 |
| Florida State | 113 | 113 | 111 | 110 | 111 | 113 | 111 | 109 | 44 | 73 | 72 | 79 |
| George Washington | 54 | 33 | 25 | 25 | 62 | 44 | 33 | 28 | 44 | 28 | 24 | 35 |
| Georgetown | 40 | 39 | 39 | 45 | 48 | 56 | 52 | 60 | 16 | 43 | 39 | 51 |
| Georgia | 97 | 99 | 107 | 111 | 106 | 106 | 109 | 112 | 108 | 105 | 104 | 105 |
| Georgia Tech | 90 | 86 | 73 | 82 | 86 | 86 | 80 | 86 | 44 | 73 | 50 | 59 |
| Guelph | 69 | 19 | 40 | 17 | 66 | 23 | 34 | 16 | 90 | 1 | 6 | 2 |
| Harvard | 16 | 16 | 17 | 20 | 26 | 25 | 23 | 29 | 8 | 18 | 15 | 7 |
| Hawaii | 74 | 54 | 57 | 86 | 54 | 33 | 38 | 57 | 42 | 65 | 66 | 111 |

## Table 14: Average, Median, and Beginning Professional Salaries in ARL University Libraries Summary of Rankings, FYs 2007–2008 to 2010–2011

| Institution | Average Salaries | | | | Median Salaries | | | | Beginning Salaries | | | |
| --- | --- | --- | --- | --- | --- | --- | --- | --- | --- | --- | --- | --- |
| FY | 2008 | 2009 | 2010 | 2011 | 2008 | 2009 | 2010 | 2011 | 2008 | 2009 | 2010 | 2011 |
| Houston | 99 | 75 | 84 | 90 | 108 | 59 | 85 | 103 | 74 | 73 | 61 | 59 |
| Howard | 108 | 110 | 114 | 109 | 93 | 101 | 114 | 111 | 107 | 108 | 104 | 113 |
| Illinois, Chicago | 89 | 83 | 81 | 84 | 84 | 85 | 86 | 89 | 9 | 28 | 24 | 35 |
| Illinois, Urbana | 62 | 57 | 56 | 47 | 68 | 61 | 61 | 51 | 26 | 41 | 34 | 21 |
| Indiana | 60 | 74 | 71 | 81 | 60 | 70 | 73 | 78 | 74 | 90 | 90 | 93 |
| Iowa | 65 | 76 | 78 | 79 | 79 | 83 | 96 | 87 | 74 | 85 | 83 | 86 |
| Iowa State | 82 | 80 | 74 | 71 | 75 | 74 | 60 | 63 | 39 | 60 | 61 | 59 |
| Johns Hopkins | 44 | 55 | 41 | 51 | 57 | 53 | 40 | 49 | 4 | 9 | 10 | 15 |
| Kansas | 86 | 85 | 90 | 88 | 82 | 87 | 98 | 92 | 74 | 16 | 7 | 73 |
| Kent State | 101 | 101 | 70 | 66 | 92 | 99 | 66 | 59 | 31 | 59 | 2 | 3 |
| Kentucky | 85 | 87 | 88 | 95 | 71 | 76 | 71 | 76 | 91 | 85 | 83 | 86 |
| Laval | 84 | 47 | 82 | 62 | 39 | 29 | 56 | 32 | 68 | 24 | 68 | 39 |
| Louisiana State | 112 | 112 | 113 | 115 | 113 | 112 | 113 | 115 | 94 | 105 | 104 | 105 |
| Louisville | 51 | 81 | 96 | 101 | 43 | 82 | 92 | 107 | 100 | 107 | 109 | 110 |
| McGill | 43 | 28 | 72 | 37 | 32 | 34 | 81 | 55 | 65 | 13 | 65 | 33 |
| McMaster | 37 | 14 | 85 | 54 | 20 | 11 | 55 | 69 | 89 | 49 | 91 | 49 |
| Manitoba | 5 | 3 | 6 | 5 | 4 | 2 | 4 | 4 | 55 | 33 | 81 | 41 |
| Maryland | 55 | 52 | 43 | 46 | 44 | 39 | 35 | 35 | 44 | 73 | 92 | 94 |
| Massachusetts | 27 | 35 | 35 | 34 | 19 | 21 | 21 | 24 | 63 | 72 | 71 | 78 |
| MIT | 25 | 24 | 24 | 23 | 29 | 25 | 22 | 25 | 5 | 6 | 4 | 12 |
| Miami | 52 | 45 | 46 | 49 | 58 | 46 | 59 | 53 | 16 | 43 | 39 | 51 |
| Michigan | 41 | 37 | 50 | 38 | 36 | 41 | 49 | 46 | 58 | 73 | 72 | 79 |
| Michigan State | 71 | 73 | 42 | 40 | 76 | 71 | 39 | 38 | 9 | 28 | 24 | 32 |
| Minnesota | 42 | 51 | 55 | 58 | 35 | 43 | 51 | 47 | 74 | 91 | 72 | 73 |
| Missouri | 95 | 106 | 94 | 99 | 104 | 110 | 91 | 94 | 91 | 91 | 92 | 94 |
| Montreal | 78 | 43 | 77 | 43 | 69 | 38 | 72 | 48 | 104 | 82 | 110 | 71 |
| Nebraska | 73 | 69 | 68 | 76 | 87 | 80 | 82 | 91 | 16 | 10 | 11 | 21 |
| New Mexico | 9 | 15 | 29 | 39 | 8 | 15 | 29 | 37 | 74 | 91 | 92 | 94 |
| New York | 4 | 13 | 12 | 21 | 21 | 27 | 26 | 30 | 2 | 3 | 3 | 4 |
| North Carolina | 34 | 58 | 51 | 74 | 37 | 52 | 50 | 68 | 44 | 51 | 50 | 59 |
| North Carolina State | 30 | 34 | 27 | 35 | 45 | 47 | 43 | 53 | 9 | 16 | 11 | 12 |
| Northwestern | 50 | 66 | 49 | 59 | 50 | 57 | 53 | 64 | 86 | 73 | 61 | 59 |
| Notre Dame | 38 | 49 | 37 | 36 | 28 | 40 | 36 | 36 | 74 | 91 | 82 | 59 |
| Ohio University | 111 | 100 | 110 | 112 | 112 | 111 | 112 | 113 | 105 | 83 | 83 | 85 |
| Ohio State | 98 | 109 | 97 | 106 | 95 | 103 | 101 | 106 | 54 | 60 | 34 | 48 |
| Oklahoma | 107 | 108 | 108 | 113 | 103 | 104 | 102 | 105 | 74 | 73 | 72 | 79 |
| Oklahoma State | 104 | 104 | 106 | 108 | 105 | 100 | 106 | 110 | 105 | 108 | 104 | 105 |
| Oregon | 103 | 103 | 95 | 91 | 102 | 98 | 90 | 88 | 108 | 91 | 92 | 94 |
| Ottawa* | N/A | N/A | N/A | 8 | N/A | N/A | N/A | 8 | N/A | N/A | N/A | 31 |

## TABLE 14: AVERAGE, MEDIAN, AND BEGINNING PROFESSIONAL SALARIES IN ARL UNIVERSITY LIBRARIES SUMMARY OF RANKINGS, FYs 2007–2008 TO 2010–2011

| Institution | Average Salaries | | | | Median Salaries | | | | Beginning Salaries | | | |
|---|---|---|---|---|---|---|---|---|---|---|---|---|
| FY | 2008 | 2009 | 2010 | 2011 | 2008 | 2009 | 2010 | 2011 | 2008 | 2009 | 2010 | 2011 |
| Pennsylvania | 66 | 68 | 62 | 65 | 64 | 65 | 58 | 62 | 39 | 67 | 59 | 86 |
| Pennsylvania State | 39 | 42 | 48 | 50 | 38 | 42 | 47 | 44 | 56 | 69 | 69 | 69 |
| Pittsburgh | 61 | 63 | 58 | 52 | 65 | 73 | 63 | 66 | 111 | 111 | 112 | 114 |
| Princeton | 13 | 17 | 13 | 14 | 18 | 22 | 18 | 18 | 16 | 10 | 1 | 1 |
| Purdue | 48 | 59 | 66 | 68 | 72 | 66 | 65 | 72 | 29 | 43 | 24 | 35 |
| Queen's | 17 | 6 | 10 | 3 | 11 | 5 | 5 | 1 | 64 | 13 | 48 | 19 |
| Rice | 72 | 82 | 80 | 73 | 83 | 89 | 93 | 73 | 85 | 103 | 108 | 103 |
| Rochester | 102 | 105 | 109 | 98 | 101 | 102 | 105 | 96 | 103 | 104 | 103 | 102 |
| Rutgers | 1 | 5 | 1 | 6 | 1 | 3 | 1 | 5 | 13 | 25 | 14 | 17 |
| Saskatchewan | 12 | 7 | 20 | 11 | 10 | 7 | 7 | 12 | 53 | 12 | 38 | 10 |
| South Carolina | 110 | 111 | 112 | 114 | 109 | 108 | 110 | 114 | 111 | 111 | 112 | 105 |
| Southern California | 22 | 27 | 23 | 29 | 33 | 36 | 31 | 33 | 16 | 20 | 17 | 26 |
| Southern Illinois | 105 | 102 | 104 | 102 | 107 | 109 | 107 | 95 | 58 | 60 | 50 | 59 |
| SUNY Albany | 77 | 56 | 89 | 80 | 77 | 75 | 75 | 67 | 94 | 101 | 101 | 101 |
| SUNY Buffalo | 58 | 38 | 30 | 30 | 52 | 37 | 27 | 31 | 16 | 43 | 39 | 35 |
| SUNY Stony Brook | 24 | 22 | 11 | 7 | 25 | 20 | 16 | 13 | 34 | 51 | 72 | 73 |
| Syracuse | 53 | 71 | 65 | 60 | 67 | 63 | 64 | 70 | N/A | 113 | N/A | 105 |
| Temple | 45 | 67 | 54 | 53 | 78 | 88 | 79 | 74 | 86 | 64 | 49 | 58 |
| Tennessee | 32 | 36 | 38 | 55 | 30 | 32 | 37 | 39 | 44 | 51 | 50 | 59 |
| Texas | 64 | 62 | 53 | 64 | 73 | 77 | 74 | 79 | 16 | 43 | 34 | 51 |
| Texas A&M | 79 | 94 | 79 | 75 | 85 | 97 | 95 | 81 | 27 | 28 | 20 | 26 |
| Texas Tech | 81 | 88 | 91 | 105 | 94 | 93 | 83 | 104 | 16 | 43 | 39 | 51 |
| Toronto | 8 | 2 | 14 | 9 | 6 | 4 | 17 | 11 | 33 | 5 | 46 | 24 |
| Tulane | 87 | 79 | 92 | 87 | 80 | 71 | 88 | 77 | 100 | 91 | 92 | 94 |
| Utah | 80 | 84 | 86 | 93 | 88 | 81 | 89 | 101 | 44 | 51 | 50 | 51 |
| Vanderbilt | 94 | 92 | 100 | 97 | 97 | 94 | 100 | 97 | 86 | 91 | 88 | 86 |
| Virginia | 36 | 44 | 47 | 44 | 58 | 68 | 67 | 58 | 34 | 51 | 50 | 59 |
| Virginia Tech | 67 | 70 | 75 | 85 | 61 | 58 | 77 | 83 | 91 | 85 | 92 | 94 |
| Washington | 63 | 64 | 59 | 70 | 70 | 69 | 69 | 82 | 58 | 66 | 67 | 77 |
| Washington State | 91 | 91 | 76 | 83 | 89 | 84 | 78 | 84 | 94 | 101 | 102 | 104 |
| Washington U.-St. Louis | 93 | 93 | 99 | 94 | 99 | 95 | 103 | 98 | 100 | 91 | 92 | 94 |
| Waterloo | 31 | 18 | 34 | 28 | 17 | 13 | 24 | 19 | 52 | 15 | 47 | 25 |
| Wayne State | 109 | 107 | 87 | 96 | 110 | 107 | 99 | 100 | 67 | 89 | 88 | 86 |
| Western Ontario | 88 | 50 | 98 | 56 | 91 | 50 | 94 | 41 | 65 | 34 | 86 | 29 |
| Wisconsin | 83 | 89 | 83 | 92 | 74 | 79 | 76 | 90 | 84 | 88 | 87 | 91 |
| Yale | 6 | 9 | 9 | 16 | 15 | 14 | 11 | 17 | 3 | 7 | 9 | 18 |
| York | 2 | 1 | 4 | 1 | 7 | 6 | 9 | 3 | 32 | 19 | 80 | 40 |

Excludes medical and law libraries.
* Ottawa became a member in 2010.

PAGE INTENTIONALLY LEFT BLANK.

# Table 15: Distribution of Professional Staff in ARL University Libraries by Salary and Position, FY 2010–2011

| Salary Intervals | Number of Staff | | | | | | | | Percent at each level[†] | | | | | | | |
|---|---|---|---|---|---|---|---|---|---|---|---|---|---|---|---|---|
| | Dir. | Assoc. Dir. | Asst. Dir. | Branch Head | Subj. Spec. | Func. Spec. | Dept. Head | Other Prof. | Dir. | Assoc. Dir. | Asst. Dir. | Branch Head | Subj. Spec. | Func. Spec. | Dept. Head | Other Prof. |
| More than 300,000 | 6 | | | | | | | | 5% | | | | | | | |
| 250,000–299,999 | 9 | | | | | | | | 8% | | | | | | | |
| 200,000–250,000 | 32 | 3 | 1 | 1 | | | 2 | | 29% | 1% | 1% | 0% | | | 0% | |
| 175,000–199,999 | 28 | 8 | 3 | | 2 | | 2 | 2 | 25% | 2% | 2% | | 0% | | 0% | 0% |
| 150,000–174,999 | 27 | 16 | 9 | 1 | | | | 2 | 25% | 5% | 5% | 0% | | | | 0% |
| 140,000–149,999 | 6 | 27 | 2 | 8 | 1 | | 8 | 1 | 5% | 8% | 1% | 0% | 0% | | 1% | 0% |
| 130,000–139,999 | | 41 | 10 | 4 | 6 | 1 | 8 | 5 | | 13% | 6% | 1% | 0% | 0% | 1% | 0% |
| 120,000–129,999 | 1 | 50 | 20 | 12 | 8 | 2 | 21 | 9 | 1% | 15% | 12% | 3% | 0% | 0% | 2% | 1% |
| 110,000–119,999 | | 59 | 21 | 16 | 23 | 22 | 46 | 18 | | 18% | 13% | 4% | 1% | 2% | 3% | 1% |
| 100,000–109,999 | | 62 | 34 | 33 | 40 | 29 | 81 | 52 | | 19% | 20% | 7% | 2% | 3% | 6% | 2% |
| 95,000–99,999 | 1 | 10 | 20 | 27 | 41 | 35 | 78 | 55 | 1% | 3% | 12% | 6% | 2% | 3% | 6% | 2% |
| 90,000–94,999 | | 15 | 9 | 29 | 56 | 29 | 84 | 36 | | 5% | 5% | 6% | 3% | 3% | 6% | 1% |
| 85,000–89,999 | | 11 | 12 | 34 | 89 | 39 | 130 | 64 | | 3% | 7% | 8% | 4% | 3% | 10% | 2% |
| 80,000–84,999 | | 12 | 8 | 43 | 114 | 69 | 149 | 94 | | 4% | 5% | 10% | 5% | 6% | 11% | 4% |
| 78,000–79,999 | | 2 | | 11 | 31 | 12 | 26 | 24 | | 1% | | 2% | 1% | 1% | 2% | 1% |
| 76,000–77,999 | | 2 | 2 | 11 | 27 | 15 | 26 | 17 | | 1% | 1% | 2% | 1% | 1% | 2% | 1% |
| 74,000–75,999 | | 1 | 2 | 18 | 55 | 31 | 57 | 54 | | 0% | 1% | 4% | 3% | 3% | 4% | 2% |
| 72,000–73,999 | | 2 | 1 | 23 | 63 | 45 | 59 | 70 | | 1% | 1% | 5% | 3% | 4% | 4% | 3% |
| 70,000–71,999 | | | 2 | 29 | 74 | 44 | 50 | 82 | | | 1% | 6% | 3% | 4% | 4% | 3% |
| 68,000–69,999 | | 1 | 1 | 18 | 67 | 50 | 51 | 86 | | 0% | 1% | 4% | 3% | 4% | 4% | 3% |
| 66,000–67,999 | | | | 22 | 90 | 58 | 54 | 105 | | | | 5% | 4% | 5% | 4% | 4% |
| 64,000–65,999 | | 1 | 3 | 18 | 84 | 49 | 48 | 98 | | 0% | 2% | 4% | 4% | 4% | 4% | 4% |
| 62,000–63,999 | | 1 | 1 | 16 | 118 | 62 | 50 | 138 | | 0% | 1% | 4% | 6% | 5% | 4% | 5% |
| 60,000–61,999 | | | 2 | 19 | 85 | 57 | 49 | 103 | | | 1% | 4% | 4% | 5% | 4% | 4% |
| 58,000–59,999 | | 1 | | 6 | 125 | 62 | 44 | 162 | | 0% | | 1% | 6% | 5% | 3% | 6% |
| 56,000–57,999 | | | 1 | 9 | 97 | 55 | 38 | 144 | | | 1% | 2% | 5% | 5% | 3% | 5% |
| 54,000–55,999 | | | 2 | 10 | 96 | 54 | 36 | 170 | | | 1% | 2% | 4% | 5% | 3% | 6% |
| 52,000–53,999 | | | | 6 | 102 | 62 | 18 | 171 | | | | 1% | 5% | 5% | 1% | 6% |
| 50,000–51,999 | | | | 8 | 119 | 58 | 33 | 173 | | | | 2% | 6% | 5% | 2% | 7% |
| 48,000–49,999 | | | 1 | 5 | 104 | 45 | 22 | 157 | | | 1% | 1% | 5% | 4% | 2% | 6% |
| 46,000–47,999 | | | | 7 | 101 | 53 | 13 | 132 | | | | 2% | 5% | 5% | 1% | 5% |
| 44,000–45,999 | | | | 2 | 101 | 56 | 12 | 119 | | | | 0% | 5% | 5% | 1% | 5% |
| 42,000–43,999 | | | 1 | 4 | 64 | 18 | 12 | 117 | | | 1% | 1% | 3% | 2% | 1% | 4% |
| 40,000–41,999 | | | | 1 | 58 | 24 | 14 | 69 | | | | 0% | 3% | 2% | 1% | 3% |
| 38,000–39,999 | | | | | 39 | 8 | 10 | 56 | | | | | 2% | 1% | 1% | 2% |
| 36,000–37,999 | | | | 1 | 23 | 1 | 2 | 25 | | | | 0% | 1% | 0% | 0% | 1% |
| 34,000–35,999 | | | | | 15 | 1 | 1 | 19 | | | | | 1% | 0% | 0% | 1% |
| less than 34,000 | | | | | 11 | 3 | 2 | 12 | | | | | 0% | 0% | 0% | 0% |
| Total | 110 | 325 | 168 | 452 | 2138 | 1149 | 1338 | 2649 | 100% | 100% | 100% | 100% | 100% | 100% | 100% | 100% |

Excludes medical and law libraries.

† A "0" percentage indicates less than one-half of one percent.

# Table 16: Distribution of Professional Staff in ARL University Libraries by Salary, Sex, and Position, FY 2010–2011

| Salary Intervals | Women Dir. | Women Assoc. Dir. | Women Asst. Dir. | Women Branch Head | Women Subj. Spec. | Women Func. Spec. | Women Dept. Head | Women Other Prof. | Men Dir. | Men Assoc. Dir. | Men Asst. Dir. | Men Branch Head | Men Subj. Spec. | Men Func. Spec. | Men Dept. Head | Men Other Prof. |
|---|---|---|---|---|---|---|---|---|---|---|---|---|---|---|---|---|
| More than 300,000 | 1 | | | | | | | | 5 | | | | | | | |
| 250,000–299,999 | 7 | | | | | | | | 2 | | | | | | | |
| 200,000–250,000 | 20 | 3 | 1 | | | | | | 12 | 4 | 1 | 1 | | | | |
| 175,000–199,999 | 16 | 4 | 3 | | | | | | 12 | 7 | 2 | | 1 | | 1 | |
| 150,000–174,999 | 16 | 9 | 1 | | 1 | | | | 11 | 10 | 6 | 1 | | | | |
| 140,000–149,999 | 4 | 17 | 4 | 3 | 1 | 1 | 1 | 1 | 2 | 14 | 1 | 1 | 1 | | 1 | 2 |
| 130,000–139,999 | | 27 | 13 | 2 | 5 | 1 | 1 | 5 | | 20 | 6 | 5 | 5 | | 4 | |
| 120,000–129,999 | 1 | 30 | 8 | 7 | 3 | | 4 | 6 | | 24 | 7 | 2 | 3 | 1 | 4 | |
| 110,000–119,999 | | 35 | 19 | 10 | 13 | 11 | 4 | 10 | | 26 | 13 | 5 | 10 | 11 | 7 | 3 |
| 100,000–109,999 | | 36 | 10 | 25 | 20 | 11 | 14 | 38 | | 3 | 15 | 6 | 20 | 18 | 17 | 8 |
| 95,000–99,999 | 1 | 7 | 6 | 15 | 19 | 18 | 29 | 40 | | 6 | 10 | 8 | 22 | 17 | 27 | 14 |
| 90,000–94,999 | | 9 | 8 | 17 | 23 | 18 | 54 | 22 | | 5 | 3 | 12 | 33 | 11 | 31 | 15 |
| 85,000–89,999 | | 6 | 5 | 25 | 37 | 25 | 47 | 45 | | 7 | 4 | 9 | 52 | 14 | 33 | 14 |
| 80,000–84,999 | | 5 | | 30 | 44 | 40 | 51 | 69 | | 1 | 3 | 13 | 70 | 29 | 50 | 19 |
| 79,000–79,999 | | 1 | 1 | 8 | 17 | 6 | 80 | 14 | | 1 | 3 | 3 | 14 | 6 | 59 | 25 |
| 78,000–78,999 | | 1 | 1 | 5 | 15 | 10 | 90 | 16 | | 1 | 1 | 6 | 12 | 5 | 7 | 10 |
| 76,000–77,999 | | | 1 | 11 | 31 | 19 | 19 | 31 | | | 1 | 7 | 24 | 12 | 10 | 1 |
| 74,000–75,999 | | 2 | 2 | 17 | 35 | 27 | 16 | 57 | | | | 6 | 28 | 18 | 21 | 23 |
| 72,000–73,999 | | | 1 | 21 | 37 | 24 | 36 | 52 | | | | 8 | 37 | 20 | 24 | 13 |
| 70,000–71,999 | | | | 15 | 35 | 30 | 35 | 56 | | | | 3 | 32 | 20 | 13 | 30 |
| 68,000–69,999 | | | 3 | 14 | 54 | 33 | 37 | 73 | | 1 | | 8 | 36 | 25 | 15 | 30 |
| 66,000–67,999 | | 1 | 1 | 12 | 47 | 30 | 36 | 72 | | | | 6 | 37 | 19 | 19 | 32 |
| 64,000–65,999 | | 1 | | 12 | 65 | 37 | 35 | 101 | | | | 4 | 53 | 25 | 18 | 26 |
| 62,000–63,999 | | | | 12 | 45 | 35 | 30 | 74 | | | 2 | 7 | 40 | 22 | 15 | 37 |
| 60,000–61,999 | | 1 | | 3 | 53 | 35 | 35 | 119 | | | | 3 | 72 | 27 | 17 | 29 |
| 58,000–59,999 | | | 1 | 4 | 54 | 27 | 32 | 109 | | | | 5 | 43 | 28 | 13 | 43 |
| 56,000–57,999 | | | 2 | 8 | 50 | 35 | 31 | 113 | | | | 2 | 46 | 19 | 19 | 35 |
| 54,000–55,999 | | | | 4 | 60 | 47 | 19 | 120 | | | | 2 | 42 | 15 | 10 | 57 |
| 52,000–53,999 | | | | 6 | 64 | 42 | 26 | 134 | | | | 2 | 55 | 16 | 9 | 51 |
| 50,000–51,999 | | | | 4 | 65 | 29 | 9 | 110 | | | | 1 | 39 | 16 | 6 | 39 |
| 48,000–49,999 | | | | 4 | 49 | 39 | 27 | 94 | | | | 3 | 52 | 14 | 5 | 47 |
| 46,000–47,999 | | | | 1 | 61 | 43 | 17 | 80 | | | | 1 | 40 | 13 | 5 | 38 |
| 44,000–45,999 | | | | 4 | 38 | 12 | 8 | 83 | | | | | 26 | 6 | 3 | 39 |
| 42,000–43,999 | | | 1 | | 33 | 15 | 9 | 49 | | | | 1 | 25 | 9 | 3 | 34 |
| 40,000–41,999 | | | | | 23 | 8 | 9 | 44 | | | | 1 | 16 | | 5 | 20 |
| 38,000–39,999 | | | | | 13 | 1 | 5 | 22 | | | | | 10 | | 1 | 12 |
| 36,000–37,999 | | | | | 11 | | 1 | 12 | | | | 1 | 4 | 1 | 1 | 3 |
| 34,000–35,999 | | | | | 7 | | | 9 | | | | | 4 | | 1 | 7 |
| less than 34,000 | | | | | 3 | | | 8 | | | | | 6 | 2 | 2 | 3 |
| **Total** | 66 | 195 | 92 | 299 | 1131 | 710 | 857 | 1888 | 44 | 130 | 76 | 153 | 1007 | 439 | 481 | 761 |

Excludes medical and law libraries.

| Position | WOMEN | | MEN | | TOTAL | |
|---|---|---|---|---|---|---|
| | Salary | No. | Salary | No. | Salary | No. |
| Director | $196,635 | 66 | $207,959 | 44 | $201,165 | 110 |
| Associate Director | 120,303 | 195 | 118,004 | 130 | 119,383 | 325 |
| Assistant Director | 101,983 | 92 | 113,257 | 76 | 107,083 | 168 |
| Head, Branch | 80,695 | 299 | 84,752 | 153 | 82,068 | 452 |
| Functional Specialist | 63,847 | 1,131 | 65,981 | 1,007 | 64,852 | 2,138 |
| Subject Specialist | 65,576 | 710 | 69,439 | 439 | 67,052 | 1,149 |
| | | | | | | |
| Dept. Head: | | | | | | |
|   Acquisitions | 76,056 | 82 | 75,563 | 30 | 75,924 | 112 |
|   Reference | 80,467 | 83 | 84,979 | 28 | 81,605 | 111 |
|   Cataloging | 76,903 | 113 | 75,455 | 41 | 76,517 | 154 |
|   Serials | 78,196 | 20 | 68,943 | 5 | 76,346 | 25 |
|   Documents/Maps | 71,437 | 34 | 72,960 | 23 | 72,052 | 57 |
|   Circulation | 74,686 | 56 | 65,272 | 28 | 71,548 | 84 |
|   Rare Books/Manuscripts | 83,595 | 44 | 83,382 | 46 | 83,486 | 90 |
|   Computer Systems | 95,783 | 26 | 90,132 | 44 | 92,231 | 70 |
|   Other | 78,011 | 399 | 80,295 | 236 | 78,860 | 635 |
| | | | | | | |
| Reference: | | | | | | |
|   Over 14 years experience | 70,864 | 404 | 69,599 | 169 | 70,491 | 573 |
|   10 to 14 years experience | 61,275 | 145 | 62,508 | 63 | 61,649 | 208 |
|   5 to 9 years experience | 56,109 | 206 | 57,283 | 74 | 56,420 | 280 |
|   Under 5 years experience | 52,470 | 152 | 51,494 | 55 | 52,211 | 207 |
| | | | | | | |
| Cataloging: | | | | | | |
|   Over 14 years experience | 66,713 | 263 | 68,155 | 125 | 67,178 | 388 |
|   10 to 14 years experience | 58,373 | 73 | 62,105 | 31 | 59,485 | 104 |
|   5 to 9 years experience | 55,073 | 99 | 57,803 | 38 | 55,830 | 137 |
|   Under 5 years experience | 50,793 | 66 | 50,748 | 31 | 50,778 | 97 |
| | | | | | | |
| Other: | | | | | | |
|   Over 14 years experience | 70,402 | 203 | 70,642 | 70 | 70,464 | 273 |
|   10 to 14 years experience | 61,901 | 86 | 60,214 | 29 | 61,476 | 115 |
|   5 to 9 years experience | 53,449 | 94 | 59,749 | 38 | 55,263 | 132 |
|   Under 5 years experience | 51,654 | 97 | 51,210 | 38 | 51,529 | 135 |
| **All Positions** | **$71,230** | **5,238** | **$74,159** | **3,091** | **$72,317** | **8,329** |

Excludes medical and law libraries. See Tables 39 and 46 for comparable figures for medical and law libraries.
Canadian salaries are expressed in US dollars. See Table 32 for salaries of Canadian librarians expressed in Canadian dollars.

## TABLE 18: NUMBER AND AVERAGE YEARS OF EXPERIENCE OF ARL UNIVERSITY LIBRARIANS BY POSITION AND SEX, FY 2010–2011

| Position | WOMEN Years | WOMEN No. | MEN Years | MEN No. | TOTAL Years | TOTAL No. |
|---|---|---|---|---|---|---|
| Director | 33.9 | 66 | 33.2 | 44 | 33.6 | 110 |
| Associate Director | 26.5 | 195 | 24.3 | 130 | 25.6 | 325 |
| Assistant Director | 25.2 | 92 | 22.9 | 76 | 24.2 | 168 |
| Head, Branch | 21.8 | 299 | 23.7 | 153 | 22.4 | 452 |
| Functional Specialist | 13.9 | 1,131 | 13.9 | 1,007 | 13.9 | 2,138 |
| Subject Specialist | 16.0 | 710 | 17.5 | 439 | 16.6 | 1,149 |
| | | | | | | |
| Dept. Head: | | | | | | |
| Acquisitions | 22.0 | 82 | 18.8 | 30 | 21.2 | 112 |
| Reference | 20.3 | 83 | 22.3 | 28 | 20.8 | 111 |
| Cataloging | 21.5 | 113 | 22.3 | 41 | 21.7 | 154 |
| Serials | 21.2 | 20 | 18.0 | 5 | 20.6 | 25 |
| Documents/Maps | 21.7 | 34 | 21.2 | 23 | 21.5 | 57 |
| Circulation | 19.7 | 56 | 18.1 | 28 | 19.2 | 84 |
| Rare Books/Manuscripts | 21.0 | 44 | 23.8 | 46 | 22.4 | 90 |
| Computer Systems | 21.8 | 26 | 17.4 | 44 | 19.0 | 70 |
| Other | 20.4 | 399 | 19.1 | 236 | 19.9 | 635 |
| | | | | | | |
| Public services | 13.5 | 230 | 12.0 | 77 | 13.1 | 307 |
| Technical services | 15.7 | 121 | 14.2 | 47 | 15.3 | 168 |
| Administration | 15.7 | 129 | 14.7 | 51 | 15.5 | 180 |
| Reference | 15.3 | 907 | 15.2 | 361 | 15.3 | 1,268 |
| Cataloger | 17.4 | 501 | 18.1 | 225 | 17.6 | 726 |
| | | | | | | |
| **All Positions** | **17.3** | **5,238** | **17.2** | **3,091** | **17.3** | **8,329** |

Excludes medical and law libraries. See Tables 40 and 47 for comparable figures for medical and law libraries.
Canadian salaries are expressed in US dollars. See Table 33 for salaries of Canadian librarians expressed in Canadian dollars.

## TABLE 19: NUMBER AND AVERAGE SALARIES OF ARL UNIVERSITY LIBRARIANS BY YEARS OF EXPERIENCE AND SEX, FY 2010–2011

| Position | WOMEN | | MEN | | TOTAL | | % OF TOTAL |
|---|---|---|---|---|---|---|---|
| | Salary | No. | Salary | No. | Salary | No. | |
| 0–3 years | $52,119 | 510 | $53,359 | 281 | $52,559 | 791 | 9% |
| 4–7 years | 55,553 | 754 | 57,412 | 408 | 56,206 | 1,162 | 14% |
| 8–11 years | 62,306 | 725 | 65,184 | 467 | 63,433 | 1,192 | 14% |
| 12–15 years | 67,850 | 632 | 70,634 | 405 | 68,937 | 1,037 | 12% |
| 16–19 years | 71,752 | 473 | 75,951 | 302 | 73,388 | 775 | 9% |
| 20–23 years | 76,649 | 560 | 77,362 | 319 | 76,908 | 879 | 11% |
| 24–27 years | 80,829 | 442 | 85,297 | 257 | 82,472 | 699 | 8% |
| 28–31 years | 86,385 | 416 | 87,248 | 245 | 86,705 | 661 | 8% |
| 32–35 years | 90,264 | 347 | 100,108 | 222 | 94,105 | 569 | 7% |
| over 35 years | 96,923 | 379 | 100,671 | 185 | 98,153 | 564 | 7% |
| **All Positions** | **$71,230** | **5,238** | **$74,159** | **3,091** | **$72,317** | **8,329** | **100%** |

Excludes medical and law libraries. See Tables 41 and 48 for comparable figures for medical and law libraries.
Canadian salaries are expressed in US dollars. See Table 34 for salaries of Canadian librarians expressed in Canadian dollars.

# TABLE 20: AVERAGE SALARIES OF ARL UNIVERSITY LIBRARIANS BY POSITION AND YEARS OF EXPERIENCE, FY 2010–2011

| Position | YEARS OF EXPERIENCE | | | | | | | | | |
|---|---|---|---|---|---|---|---|---|---|---|
| | 0–3 years | 4–7 years | 8–11 years | 12–15 years | 16–19 years | 20–23 years | 24–27 years | 28–31 years | 32–35 years | over 35 years |
| Director | ‡ | . | . | ‡ | ‡ | $166,747 | $198,652 | $193,532 | $203,773 | $204,661 |
| Associate Director | ‡ | $100,582 | $98,867 | $107,348 | $106,436 | 121,927 | 124,455 | 122,930 | 120,326 | 131,460 |
| Assistant Director | ‡ | 96,620 | 94,353 | 93,925 | 113,748 | 109,721 | 107,734 | 109,251 | 111,271 | 114,338 |
| Head, Branch | $63,335 | 60,671 | 70,119 | 73,900 | 77,900 | 81,293 | 85,350 | 82,722 | 95,823 | 101,021 |
| Functional Specialist | 52,385 | 56,401 | 62,155 | 67,075 | 68,416 | 71,498 | 76,008 | 78,275 | 80,307 | 80,946 |
| Subject Specialist | 51,079 | 54,917 | 62,735 | 65,667 | 69,457 | 73,268 | 74,817 | 79,574 | 83,053 | 83,111 |
| Dept. Head: | | | | | | | | | | |
| Acquisitions | 59,851 | 60,364 | 66,739 | 73,267 | 78,200 | 76,587 | 86,098 | 75,367 | 81,867 | 91,270 |
| Reference | ‡ | 66,540 | 75,544 | 79,146 | 80,933 | 83,827 | 83,622 | 81,178 | 91,291 | 94,216 |
| Cataloging | ‡ | 58,459 | 64,890 | 69,560 | 72,421 | 76,899 | 82,383 | 80,695 | 96,823 | 80,084 |
| Serials | ‡ | . | ‡ | ‡ | 86,643 | 74,901 | ‡ | ‡ | ‡ | ‡ |
| Documents/Maps | ‡ | 53,589 | 58,251 | 73,308 | 71,972 | 64,824 | 76,468 | ‡ | ‡ | 83,906 |
| Circulation | 55,182 | 59,401 | 61,050 | 65,506 | 79,869 | 74,960 | 72,163 | 93,490 | 78,506 | 80,079 |
| Rare Books/Manuscripts | ‡ | 81,387 | 74,231 | 71,094 | 86,724 | 80,020 | 92,164 | 82,690 | 84,123 | 101,984 |
| Computer Systems | ‡ | 85,954 | 98,118 | 87,986 | 93,507 | 81,216 | 89,596 | 101,668 | 105,911 | . |
| Other | 54,750 | 63,064 | 68,761 | 76,798 | 79,492 | 78,122 | 86,131 | 86,469 | 91,855 | 94,374 |
| Public services | 49,702 | 50,993 | 56,488 | 61,836 | 64,491 | 62,872 | 60,707 | 66,554 | 66,293 | 71,530 |
| Technical services | 46,958 | 53,944 | 60,996 | 60,300 | 72,079 | 60,161 | 68,408 | 68,407 | 75,198 | 70,692 |
| Administration | 58,367 | 59,635 | 62,162 | 67,372 | 73,035 | 77,651 | 90,884 | 80,974 | 84,005 | 97,644 |
| Reference | 51,706 | 54,199 | 60,725 | 62,056 | 64,012 | 70,115 | 70,972 | 75,176 | 70,833 | 79,751 |
| Cataloger | 50,079 | 53,891 | 57,990 | 59,819 | 63,019 | 65,954 | 67,208 | 67,623 | 70,342 | 73,108 |
| **All Positions:** | | | | | | | | | | |
| Average Salary | $52,559 | $56,206 | $63,433 | $68,937 | $73,388 | $76,908 | $82,472 | $86,705 | $93,658 | $98,153 |
| Number of Positions | 791 | 1,162 | 1,192 | 1,037 | 775 | 879 | 699 | 661 | 569 | 564 |

Years of experience reflect total professional experience.

Excludes medical and law libraries.

Canadian salaries are expressed in US dollars.

‡ Salary data are not published when fewer than four individuals are involved.

. No positions reported in this category.

## TABLE 21: NUMBER AND AVERAGE SALARIES OF ARL UNIVERSITY LIBRARIANS BY POSITION AND TYPE OF INSTITUTION, FY 2010–2011

| Position | CANADIAN (16) Salary | No. | PRIVATE (31) Salary | No. | PUBLIC (68) Salary | No. | TOTAL (115) Salary | No. |
|---|---|---|---|---|---|---|---|---|
| Director | $167,242 | 16 | $236,090 | 29 | $193,933 | 65 | $201,165 | 110 |
| Associate Director | 121,022 | 46 | 130,596 | 92 | 113,464 | 187 | 119,383 | 325 |
| Assistant Director | 102,515 | 17 | 108,861 | 79 | 106,211 | 72 | 107,083 | 168 |
| Head, Branch | 97,517 | 62 | 84,910 | 112 | 77,478 | 278 | 82,068 | 452 |
| Functional Specialist | 75,411 | 167 | 68,188 | 831 | 60,873 | 1,140 | 64,852 | 2,138 |
| Subject Specialist | 71,887 | 130 | 67,890 | 398 | 65,502 | 621 | 67,052 | 1,149 |
| | | | | | | | | |
| Dept. Head: | | | | | | | | |
| Acquisitions | 91,481 | 16 | 74,494 | 34 | 72,694 | 62 | 75,924 | 112 |
| Reference | 90,489 | 12 | 82,901 | 42 | 78,779 | 57 | 81,605 | 111 |
| Cataloging | 92,377 | 12 | 78,882 | 59 | 72,543 | 83 | 76,517 | 154 |
| Serials | 92,313 | 4 | 73,269 | 11 | 73,342 | 10 | 76,346 | 25 |
| Documents/Maps | 96,019 | 9 | 69,386 | 16 | 66,644 | 32 | 72,052 | 57 |
| Circulation | 78,883 | 14 | 72,519 | 22 | 68,964 | 48 | 71,548 | 84 |
| Rare Books/Manuscripts | 91,750 | 7 | 82,873 | 32 | 82,736 | 51 | 83,486 | 90 |
| Computer Systems | 94,836 | 9 | 91,124 | 18 | 92,149 | 43 | 92,231 | 70 |
| Other | 91,453 | 68 | 80,968 | 177 | 75,707 | 390 | 78,860 | 635 |
| | | | | | | | | |
| Reference: | | | | | | | | |
| Over 14 years experience | 93,383 | 93 | 66,581 | 138 | 65,843 | 342 | 70,491 | 573 |
| 10 to 14 years experience | 75,721 | 38 | 61,144 | 59 | 57,099 | 111 | 61,649 | 208 |
| 5 to 9 years experience | 69,092 | 63 | 56,169 | 60 | 51,430 | 157 | 56,420 | 280 |
| Under 5 years experience | 62,739 | 59 | 50,562 | 43 | 46,970 | 105 | 52,211 | 207 |
| | | | | | | | | |
| Cataloging: | | | | | | | | |
| Over 14 years experience | 82,259 | 34 | 67,321 | 155 | 64,490 | 199 | 67,178 | 388 |
| 10 to 14 years experience | 71,448 | 7 | 61,653 | 50 | 55,397 | 47 | 59,485 | 104 |
| 5 to 9 years experience | 70,778 | 12 | 58,227 | 63 | 50,502 | 62 | 55,830 | 137 |
| Under 5 years experience | 66,359 | 9 | 51,810 | 45 | 46,437 | 43 | 50,778 | 97 |
| | | | | | | | | |
| Other: | | | | | | | | |
| Over 14 years experience | 82,045 | 20 | 71,863 | 81 | 68,458 | 172 | 70,464 | 273 |
| 10 to 14 years experience | 69,831 | 12 | 68,269 | 28 | 57,603 | 75 | 61,476 | 115 |
| 5 to 9 years experience | 68,077 | 7 | 61,578 | 42 | 50,986 | 83 | 55,263 | 132 |
| Under 5 years experience | 59,992 | 14 | 55,542 | 42 | 47,896 | 79 | 51,529 | 135 |
| **All Positions** | **$83,424** | **957** | **$73,955** | **2,758** | **$69,034** | **4,614** | **$72,317** | **8,329** |

Excludes medical and law libraries.
Canadian salaries are expressed in US dollars. See Tables 31–34 for salaries of Canadian librarians expressed in Canadian dollars.
( ) Indicates the number of ARL libraries in each category.

## TABLE 22: YEARS OF EXPERIENCE OF ARL UNIVERSITY LIBRARIANS BY POSITION AND TYPE OF INSTITUTION, FY 2010–2011

| Position | CANADIAN (16) Years | No. | PRIVATE (31) Years | No. | PUBLIC (68) Years | No. | TOTAL (115) Years | No. |
|---|---|---|---|---|---|---|---|---|
| Director | 32.6 | 16 | 33.5 | 29 | 34.0 | 65 | 33.6 | 110 |
| Associate Director | 23.7 | 46 | 26.3 | 92 | 25.7 | 187 | 25.6 | 325 |
| Assistant Director | 23.7 | 17 | 23.7 | 79 | 24.8 | 72 | 24.2 | 168 |
| Head, Branch | 20.8 | 62 | 22.9 | 112 | 22.6 | 278 | 22.4 | 452 |
| Functional Specialist | 14.5 | 167 | 14.0 | 831 | 13.8 | 1,140 | 13.9 | 2,138 |
| Subject Specialist | 13.9 | 130 | 17.3 | 398 | 16.7 | 621 | 16.6 | 1,149 |
| | | | | | | | | |
| Dept. Head: | | | | | | | | |
| Acquisitions | 19.1 | 16 | 20.3 | 34 | 22.2 | 62 | 21.2 | 112 |
| Reference | 18.1 | 12 | 20.9 | 42 | 21.3 | 57 | 20.8 | 111 |
| Cataloging | 25.4 | 12 | 21.4 | 59 | 21.4 | 83 | 21.7 | 154 |
| Serials | 22.8 | 4 | 21.2 | 11 | 19.0 | 10 | 20.6 | 25 |
| Documents/Maps | 24.6 | 9 | 21.3 | 16 | 20.8 | 32 | 21.5 | 57 |
| Circulation | 19.1 | 14 | 18.4 | 22 | 19.5 | 48 | 19.2 | 84 |
| Rare Books/Manuscripts | 23.3 | 7 | 20.6 | 32 | 23.5 | 51 | 22.4 | 90 |
| Computer Systems | 19.2 | 9 | 16.8 | 18 | 19.9 | 43 | 19.0 | 70 |
| Other | 19.7 | 68 | 20.7 | 177 | 19.6 | 390 | 19.9 | 635 |
| | | | | | | | | |
| Reference: | | | | | | | | |
| Over 14 years experience | 25.7 | 93 | 26.1 | 138 | 24.9 | 342 | 25.3 | 573 |
| 10 to 14 years experience | 11.4 | 38 | 11.9 | 59 | 11.5 | 111 | 11.6 | 208 |
| 5 to 9 years experience | 7.0 | 63 | 7.0 | 60 | 6.9 | 157 | 6.9 | 280 |
| Under 5 years experience | 2.3 | 59 | 2.7 | 43 | 2.6 | 105 | 2.5 | 207 |
| | | | | | | | | |
| Cataloging: | | | | | | | | |
| Over 14 years experience | 29.8 | 34 | 26.1 | 155 | 26.4 | 199 | 26.6 | 388 |
| 10 to 14 years experience | 12.9 | 7 | 11.6 | 50 | 12.1 | 47 | 11.9 | 104 |
| 5 to 9 years experience | 7.3 | 12 | 7.0 | 63 | 7.1 | 62 | 7.1 | 137 |
| Under 5 years experience | 2.1 | 9 | 2.6 | 45 | 3.0 | 43 | 2.7 | 97 |
| | | | | | | | | |
| Other: | | | | | | | | |
| Over 14 years experience | 24.0 | 20 | 25.3 | 81 | 24.7 | 172 | 24.8 | 273 |
| 10 to 14 years experience | 10.9 | 12 | 11.9 | 28 | 11.8 | 75 | 11.8 | 115 |
| 5 to 9 years experience | 7.1 | 7 | 6.7 | 42 | 6.8 | 83 | 6.8 | 132 |
| Under 5 years experience | 2.8 | 14 | 2.5 | 42 | 2.8 | 79 | 2.7 | 135 |
| | | | | | | | | |
| **All Positions** | **16.6** | **957** | **17.2** | **2,758** | **17.4** | **4,614** | **17.3** | **8,329** |

Excludes medical and law libraries.
( ) Indicates the number of ARL libraries in each category.

## TABLE 23: NUMBER AND AVERAGE SALARIES OF ARL UNIVERSITY LIBRARIANS BY POSITION AND SIZE OF PROFESSIONAL STAFF, FY 2010–2011

| Position | STAFF OVER 110 (15)† Salary | No. | STAFF 75–110 (17) Salary | No. | STAFF 50–74 (48) Salary | No. | STAFF 13–49 (35)‡ Salary | No. |
|---|---|---|---|---|---|---|---|---|
| Director | $244,844 | 14 | $222,538 | 17 | $195,873 | 46 | $178,999 | 33 |
| Associate Director | 136,680 | 65 | 121,478 | 72 | 113,583 | 119 | 110,906 | 69 |
| Assistant Director | 119,265 | 38 | 102,412 | 40 | 105,584 | 71 | 98,156 | 19 |
| Head, Branch | 85,564 | 135 | 83,668 | 78 | 80,370 | 169 | 77,643 | 70 |
| Functional Specialist | 67,381 | 749 | 67,980 | 416 | 61,896 | 710 | 60,680 | 263 |
| Subject Specialist | 68,842 | 349 | 70,983 | 231 | 65,264 | 469 | 60,107 | 100 |
| | | | | | | | | |
| Dept. Head: | | | | | | | | |
| Acquisitions | 74,776 | 20 | 86,294 | 16 | 73,829 | 48 | 74,410 | 28 |
| Reference | 91,147 | 21 | 83,027 | 23 | 77,032 | 35 | 79,322 | 32 |
| Cataloging | 83,135 | 46 | 80,891 | 23 | 70,335 | 54 | 74,221 | 31 |
| Serials | 80,443 | 7 | 71,642 | 2 | 78,756 | 9 | 70,493 | 7 |
| Documents/Maps | 81,922 | 10 | 67,847 | 9 | 74,261 | 20 | 66,215 | 18 |
| Circulation | 81,209 | 18 | 74,503 | 13 | 68,097 | 36 | 66,368 | 17 |
| Rare Books/Manuscripts | 95,439 | 11 | 90,010 | 18 | 77,934 | 33 | 81,139 | 28 |
| Computer Systems | 109,147 | 10 | 106,409 | 9 | 85,048 | 33 | 88,912 | 18 |
| Other | 83,885 | 162 | 80,971 | 116 | 76,401 | 252 | 74,674 | 105 |
| | | | | | | | | |
| Reference: | 70,791 | 109 | 69,528 | 85 | 71,070 | 209 | 70,068 | 170 |
| Over 14 years experience | | | | | | | | |
| 10 to 14 years experience | 65,016 | 49 | 61,557 | 33 | 60,073 | 66 | 60,683 | 60 |
| 5 to 9 years experience | 60,357 | 51 | 56,494 | 55 | 57,949 | 91 | 52,274 | 83 |
| Under 5 years experience | 56,246 | 38 | 49,955 | 31 | 53,646 | 88 | 48,016 | 50 |
| | | | | | | | | |
| Cataloging: | 71,998 | 126 | 64,461 | 82 | 63,710 | 130 | 68,504 | 50 |
| Over 14 years experience | | | | | | | | |
| 10 to 14 years experience | 63,613 | 44 | 58,514 | 20 | 56,612 | 26 | 53,236 | 14 |
| 5 to 9 years experience | 60,065 | 51 | 55,542 | 27 | 52,290 | 40 | 52,328 | 19 |
| Under 5 years experience | 55,209 | 32 | 47,245 | 25 | 51,637 | 27 | 44,883 | 13 |
| | | | | | | | | |
| Other: | 72,589 | 81 | 71,473 | 62 | 69,367 | 88 | 67,173 | 42 |
| Over 14 years experience | | | | | | | | |
| 10 to 14 years experience | 65,835 | 42 | 59,654 | 33 | 61,601 | 24 | 53,603 | 16 |
| 5 to 9 years experience | 55,556 | 46 | 58,054 | 25 | 55,761 | 36 | 51,215 | 25 |
| Under 5 years experience | 53,512 | 52 | 54,252 | 25 | 50,153 | 40 | 45,079 | 18 |
| **All Positions** | **$73,863** | **2,376** | **$74,158** | **1,586** | **$71,110** | **2,969** | **$70,164** | **1,398** |

Excludes medical and law libraries.

Canadian salaries are expressed in US dollars. See Tables 31–34 for salaries of Canadian librarians expressed in Canadian dollars.

( ) Indicates the number of ARL libraries in each category.

† In 1995–1996 and earlier, the first column of this table reported staff over 124; in 1996–1998 over 120; in 1998–1999 over 115; and since 1999–2000, over 110.

‡ No ARL library has fewer than 13 professional staff members.

# TABLE 24: YEARS OF EXPERIENCE OF ARL UNIVERSITY LIBRARIANS BY POSITION AND SIZE OF PROFESSIONAL STAFF, FY 2010–2011

| Position | STAFF OVER 110 (15)† Years | No. | STAFF 75–110 (17) Years | No. | STAFF 50–74 (48) Years | No. | STAFF 13–49 (35)‡ Years | No. |
|---|---|---|---|---|---|---|---|---|
| Director | 35.6 | 14 | 34.8 | 17 | 31.7 | 46 | 34.9 | 33 |
| Associate Director | 25.8 | 65 | 26.4 | 72 | 24.9 | 119 | 25.8 | 69 |
| Assistant Director | 25.4 | 38 | 22.2 | 40 | 24.7 | 71 | 24.1 | 19 |
| Head, Branch | 23.0 | 135 | 22.8 | 78 | 21.6 | 169 | 22.8 | 70 |
| Functional Specialist | 13.5 | 749 | 13.8 | 416 | 14.3 | 710 | 14.2 | 263 |
| Subject Specialist | 15.9 | 349 | 17.0 | 231 | 17.4 | 469 | 14.2 | 100 |
| | | | | | | | | |
| Dept. Head: | | | | | | | | |
| Acquisitions | 20.7 | 20 | 23.2 | 16 | 20.6 | 48 | 21.4 | 28 |
| Reference | 22.2 | 21 | 22.0 | 23 | 19.4 | 35 | 20.5 | 32 |
| Cataloging | 22.9 | 46 | 22.9 | 23 | 21.6 | 54 | 19.3 | 31 |
| Serials | 25.9 | 7 | 25.0 | 2 | 18.3 | 9 | 16.9 | 7 |
| Documents/Maps | 22.4 | 10 | 18.8 | 9 | 25.8 | 20 | 17.6 | 18 |
| Circulation | 21.7 | 18 | 18.8 | 13 | 18.4 | 36 | 18.3 | 17 |
| Rare Books/Manuscripts | 20.5 | 11 | 23.9 | 18 | 21.1 | 33 | 23.8 | 28 |
| Computer Systems | 21.9 | 10 | 16.9 | 9 | 17.8 | 33 | 20.6 | 18 |
| Other | 21.8 | 162 | 19.1 | 116 | 19.1 | 252 | 19.8 | 105 |
| | | | | | | | | |
| Reference: | | | | | | | | |
| Over 14 years experience | 26.6 | 109 | 25.3 | 85 | 24.9 | 209 | 25.0 | 170 |
| 10 to 14 years experience | 11.8 | 49 | 11.7 | 33 | 11.5 | 66 | 11.6 | 60 |
| 5 to 9 years experience | 7.3 | 51 | 7.0 | 55 | 6.9 | 91 | 6.7 | 83 |
| Under 5 years experience | 2.4 | 38 | 2.4 | 31 | 2.5 | 88 | 2.6 | 50 |
| | | | | | | | | |
| Cataloging: | | | | | | | | |
| Over 14 years experience | 27.0 | 126 | 24.4 | 82 | 27.5 | 130 | 26.6 | 50 |
| 10 to 14 years experience | 11.6 | 44 | 11.7 | 20 | 12.3 | 26 | 12.2 | 14 |
| 5 to 9 years experience | 7.0 | 51 | 7.0 | 27 | 6.9 | 40 | 7.8 | 19 |
| Under 5 years experience | 3.0 | 32 | 2.3 | 25 | 2.7 | 27 | 2.8 | 13 |
| | | | | | | | | |
| Other: | | | | | | | | |
| Over 14 years experience | 24.9 | 81 | 25.2 | 62 | 24.4 | 88 | 24.9 | 42 |
| 10 to 14 years experience | 11.7 | 42 | 11.7 | 33 | 11.9 | 24 | 11.8 | 16 |
| 5 to 9 years experience | 6.6 | 46 | 6.6 | 25 | 6.8 | 36 | 7.2 | 25 |
| Under 5 years experience | 2.7 | 52 | 2.6 | 25 | 2.9 | 40 | 2.4 | 18 |
| | | | | | | | | |
| **All Positions** | **16.8** | **2,376** | **17.1** | **1,586** | **17.6** | **2,969** | **17.6** | **1,398** |

Excludes medical and law libraries.

( ) Indicates the number of ARL libraries in each category.

† In 1995–1996 and earlier, the first column of this table reported staff over 124; in 1996–1998 over 120; in 1998–1999 over 115; and since 1999–2000, over 110.

‡ No ARL library has fewer than 13 professional staff members.

# TABLE 25: AVERAGE SALARIES OF ARL UNIVERSITY LIBRARIANS by POSITION AND GEOGRAPHIC REGION, FY 2010–2011

| Position | Northeast | | North Central | | South | | | West | | Canada | Total |
| --- | --- | --- | --- | --- | --- | --- | --- | --- | --- | --- | --- |
| | New England | Middle Atlantic | East North Central | West North Central | South Atlantic | East South Central | West South Central | Mountain | Pacific | | |
| | (9) | (14) | (17) | (7) | (18) | (6) | (9) | (7) | (12) | (16) | (115) |
| Director | $214,633 | $245,168 | $206,502 | $190,608 | $214,713 | $170,565 | $197,325 | $174,662 | $202,292 | $167,242 | $201,165 |
| Associate Director | 135,355 | 131,676 | 109,698 | 111,519 | 122,802 | 97,039 | 106,691 | 106,891 | 124,759 | 121,022 | 119,383 |
| Assistant Director | 105,082 | 117,902 | 95,168 | 103,179 | 108,084 | 97,579 | 98,232 | 110,953 | 104,564 | 102,515 | 107,083 |
| Head, Branch | 90,288 | 89,024 | 76,547 | 75,100 | 71,716 | 73,229 | 75,779 | 80,720 | 83,697 | 97,517 | 82,068 |
| Functional Specialist | 73,727 | 66,318 | 59,094 | 64,176 | 61,900 | 52,483 | 57,074 | 61,224 | 66,964 | 75,411 | 64,852 |
| Subject Specialist | 74,203 | 69,001 | 63,507 | 61,418 | 59,137 | 58,525 | 55,882 | 63,192 | 74,880 | 71,887 | 67,052 |
| **Dept. Head:** | | | | | | | | | | | |
| Acquisitions | 81,666 | 76,650 | 70,510 | 67,440 | 71,576 | 63,430 | 64,850 | 76,186 | 85,849 | 91,481 | 75,924 |
| Reference | 93,148 | 82,191 | 79,088 | 73,650 | 76,424 | ‡ | 72,408 | 80,113 | 83,435 | 90,489 | 81,605 |
| Cataloging | 89,501 | 76,987 | 71,405 | 70,564 | 66,648 | 59,583 | 74,852 | 77,150 | 83,968 | 92,377 | 76,517 |
| Serials | ‡ | ‡ | ‡ | . | 71,031 | ‡ | ‡ | ‡ | ‡ | 92,313 | 76,346 |
| Documents/Maps | ‡ | 73,146 | 64,187 | 67,339 | 61,210 | ‡ | 64,388 | ‡ | ‡ | 96,019 | 72,052 |
| Circulation | 79,232 | 71,997 | 72,105 | 54,814 | 70,326 | ‡ | 60,292 | ‡ | 81,958 | 78,883 | 71,548 |
| Rare Books/Manuscripts | 91,587 | 89,386 | 82,999 | 79,302 | 85,589 | 75,958 | 67,044 | 76,333 | 83,817 | 91,750 | 83,486 |
| Computer Systems | 105,389 | 93,020 | 83,528 | ‡ | 91,537 | ‡ | 92,218 | 86,999 | 93,083 | 94,836 | 92,231 |
| Other | 85,704 | 82,400 | 79,863 | 64,489 | 73,429 | 70,390 | 65,819 | 71,887 | 84,864 | 91,453 | 78,860 |
| **Reference:** | | | | | | | | | | | |
| Over 14 years experience | 72,418 | 68,689 | 66,723 | 58,084 | 63,681 | 61,694 | 53,069 | 61,883 | 72,588 | 93,383 | 70,491 |
| 10 to 14 years experience | 64,907 | 59,516 | 59,648 | 54,599 | 56,570 | 57,415 | 49,771 | 54,713 | 58,094 | 75,721 | 61,649 |
| 5 to 9 years experience | 67,631 | 54,083 | 52,573 | 52,974 | 51,792 | 49,317 | 46,583 | 50,337 | 51,933 | 69,092 | 56,420 |
| Under 5 years experience | 57,312 | 50,001 | 48,749 | 46,942 | 47,471 | 44,928 | 39,390 | 45,924 | 48,087 | 62,739 | 52,211 |
| **Cataloging:** | | | | | | | | | | | |
| Over 14 years experience | 75,265 | 64,833 | 61,217 | 59,293 | 61,398 | 58,141 | 56,668 | 63,115 | 73,482 | 82,259 | 67,178 |
| 10 to 14 years experience | 66,397 | 56,467 | 54,990 | ‡ | 53,997 | ‡ | 51,555 | 55,954 | 58,138 | 71,448 | 59,485 |
| 5 to 9 years experience | 61,790 | 56,968 | 50,381 | 47,633 | 51,610 | 45,317 | 54,225 | 49,319 | 53,220 | 70,778 | 55,830 |
| Under 5 years experience | 56,813 | 45,313 | 47,350 | ‡ | 43,417 | 44,778 | 46,392 | 46,186 | 50,227 | 66,359 | 50,778 |
| **Other:** | | | | | | | | | | | |
| Over 14 years experience | 75,756 | 80,128 | 69,924 | 57,528 | 64,160 | 67,478 | 59,914 | 63,229 | 77,191 | 82,045 | 70,464 |
| 10 to 14 years experience | 73,745 | 58,117 | 58,503 | 55,454 | 63,404 | ‡ | 54,971 | 53,635 | 67,435 | 69,831 | 61,476 |
| 5 to 9 years experience | 62,806 | 61,203 | 49,613 | 55,572 | 54,219 | 53,101 | 49,016 | 50,553 | 57,183 | 68,077 | 55,263 |
| Under 5 years experience | 61,491 | 54,526 | 46,520 | 52,039 | 49,847 | ‡ | 45,973 | 49,086 | ‡ | 59,992 | 51,529 |
| **All Positions:** | | | | | | | | | | | |
| Average Salary | $77,452 | $75,466 | $67,455 | $66,187 | $69,020 | $62,842 | $63,672 | $67,835 | $75,823 | $83,424 | $72,317 |
| No. of Staff | 1,029 | 1,218 | 1,360 | 450 | 1,124 | 303 | 592 | 404 | 892 | 957 | 8,329 |

Excludes medical and law libraries.
Canadian salaries are expressed in US dollars.
( ) Indicates number of ARL libraries included.
‡ Salary data are not published when fewer than four individuals are involved.

## ARL University Libraries by Geographic Region

| Region | Number of Libraries | ARL University Libraries Included | States/Provinces Included |
|---|---|---|---|
| **Northeast** | | | |
| 1. New England | 9 | Boston University, Boston College, Brown, Connecticut, Dartmouth, Harvard, Massachusetts Institute of Technology, Massachusetts, Yale | Conn., Mass., Me., N.H., R.I., Vt. |
| 2. Middle Atlantic | 14 | Columbia; Cornell; New York; Pennsylvania; Pennsylvania State; Pittsburgh; Princeton; Rochester; Rutgers; State University of New York: Albany, Buffalo, Stony Brook; Syracuse; Temple | N.J., N.Y., Pa. |
| **North Central** | | | |
| 3. East North Central | 17 | Case Western Reserve, Chicago, Cincinnati, Illinois-Chicago, Illinois-Urbana, Indiana, Kent State, Michigan, Michigan State, Notre Dame, Northwestern, Ohio University, Ohio State, Purdue, Southern Illinois, Wayne State, Wisconsin | Ill., Ind., Mich., Ohio, Wis. |
| 4. West North Central | 7 | Iowa, Iowa State, Kansas, Minnesota, Missouri, Nebraska, Washington U.-St. Louis | Iowa, Kan., Minn., Mo., Neb., N. Dak., S. Dak. |
| **South** | | | |
| 5. South Atlantic | 18 | Delaware, Duke, Emory, Florida, Florida State, Georgia, Georgia Tech., Georgetown, George Washington, Howard, Johns Hopkins, Maryland, Miami, North Carolina, North Carolina State, South Carolina, Virginia, Virginia Tech | Del., DC, Fla., Ga., Md., N.C., S.C., Va., W. Va. |
| 6. East South Central | 6 | Alabama, Auburn, Kentucky, Louisville, Tennessee, Vanderbilt | Ala., Ky., Miss., Tenn. |
| 7. West South Central | 9 | Houston, Louisiana State, Oklahoma, Oklahoma State, Rice, Texas, Texas A&M, Texas Tech, Tulane | Ark., La., Okla., Tex. |
| **West** | | | |
| 8. Mountain | 7 | Arizona, Arizona State, Brigham Young, Colorado, Colorado State, New Mexico, Utah | Ariz., Colo., Idaho, Mont., Nev., N. Mex., Utah, Wyo. |
| 9. Pacific | 12 | University of California: Berkeley, Davis, Irvine, Los Angeles, Riverside, San Diego, Santa Barbara; Hawaii; Oregon; Southern California; Washington; Washington State | Alaska, Calif., Hawaii, Ore., Wash. |
| **Canada** | 16 | Alberta, British Columbia, Calgary, Guelph, Laval, McGill, McMaster, Manitoba, Montreal, Ottawa, Queen's, Saskatchewan, Toronto, Waterloo, Western Ontario, York | Alta., B.C., Man., N. Br., Newf., N.S., Ont., P.E.I., Que., Sask. |

Regions are based on the classification used by the US Bureau of the Census in tabulations of the Current Population Survey.

# US ARL University Libraries

## Tables 26–30

## TABLE 26: AVERAGE SALARIES OF US ARL UNIVERSITY LIBRARIANS BY POSITION AND YEARS OF EXPERIENCE, FY 2010–2011

| Position | 0–3 years | 4–7 years | 8–11 years | 12–15 years | 16–19 years | 20–23 years | 24–27 years | 28–31 years | 32–35 years | over 35 years |
|---|---|---|---|---|---|---|---|---|---|---|
| Director | ‡ | . | . | ‡ | ‡ | ‡ | $206,556 | $203,640 | $211,876 | $207,742 |
| Associate Director | ‡ | ‡ | $96,883 | $106,210 | $107,388 | $121,503 | 122,256 | 122,957 | 120,199 | 131,115 |
| Assistant Director | ‡ | $96,620 | 94,726 | 94,481 | 115,114 | 112,744 | 108,936 | 109,249 | 111,803 | 112,107 |
| Head, Branch | $49,375 | 56,338 | 66,623 | 71,214 | 76,862 | 79,743 | 82,826 | 78,928 | 94,157 | 96,660 |
| Functional Specialist | 51,339 | 55,695 | 61,368 | 66,315 | 67,010 | 70,818 | 74,990 | 77,669 | 78,976 | 80,171 |
| Subject Specialist | 49,972 | 54,129 | 61,823 | 64,897 | 69,023 | 72,162 | 74,060 | 77,544 | 81,970 | 81,402 |
| **Dept. Head:** | | | | | | | | | | |
| Acquisitions | 59,183 | 60,364 | 63,698 | 67,893 | 76,866 | 72,796 | 81,159 | 74,183 | 81,867 | 86,842 |
| Reference | ‡ | 63,150 | 74,251 | 78,754 | 81,586 | 82,146 | 82,259 | 81,178 | 82,925 | 94,216 |
| Cataloging | ‡ | 58,459 | 64,890 | 69,082 | 71,425 | 75,719 | 81,559 | 78,881 | 95,766 | 80,084 |
| Serials | ‡ | . | ‡ | ‡ | 86,643 | 71,012 | . | ‡ | ‡ | ‡ |
| Documents/Maps | ‡ | 53,589 | 58,251 | 71,000 | 59,224 | 64,824 | 72,286 | ‡ | ‡ | 76,984 |
| Circulation | 52,621 | 59,401 | 60,280 | 63,214 | 79,869 | 68,270 | 72,520 | 89,817 | 78,590 | 80,778 |
| Rare Books/Manuscripts | ‡ | ‡ | 74,231 | 71,094 | 86,724 | 78,073 | 92,164 | 81,112 | 84,123 | 103,218 |
| Computer Systems | ‡ | 72,140 | 98,118 | 89,357 | 94,268 | 81,896 | 91,958 | 100,075 | 106,113 | . |
| Other | 49,994 | 60,471 | 67,516 | 76,062 | 78,403 | 77,402 | 83,857 | 84,414 | 90,848 | 92,704 |
| Public services | 48,668 | 50,128 | 55,856 | 60,756 | 64,491 | 61,809 | 61,795 | 66,554 | 66,293 | 71,530 |
| Technical services | 46,600 | 53,944 | 59,698 | 59,181 | 64,982 | 59,738 | 67,554 | 63,974 | 75,198 | 70,692 |
| Administration | 57,742 | 57,855 | 62,349 | 65,659 | 73,035 | 73,766 | 96,785 | 80,974 | 82,114 | 97,647 |
| Reference | 48,015 | 50,312 | 57,188 | 58,418 | 60,810 | 65,105 | 66,019 | 71,874 | 68,853 | 71,867 |
| Cataloger | 48,255 | 52,694 | 56,907 | 58,748 | 62,533 | 64,929 | 65,781 | 66,701 | 68,292 | 70,326 |
| **All Positions:** | | | | | | | | | | |
| Average Salary | $50,879 | $54,611 | $62,003 | $67,651 | $71,924 | $75,122 | $80,563 | $84,783 | $93,536 | $96,114 |
| Number of Staff | 653 | 1,031 | 1,056 | 947 | 695 | 781 | 616 | 588 | 508 | 497 |

Excludes Canadian libraries.
Excludes medical and law libraries.
‡ Salary data are not published when fewer than four individuals are involved.
. No positions reported in this category.

## TABLE 27: NUMBER AND AVERAGE SALARIES OF MINORITY US ARL UNIVERSITY LIBRARIANS BY POSITION AND SEX, FY 2010–2011

| Position | WOMEN Salary | No. | MEN Salary | No. | TOTAL Salary | No. |
|---|---|---|---|---|---|---|
| Director | ‡ | 5 | ‡ | 2 | $167,134 | 7 |
| Associate Director | 121,755 | 17 | $123,541 | 4 | 122,096 | 21 |
| Assistant Director | 110,529 | 6 | 115,346 | 7 | 113,123 | 13 |
| Head, Branch | 70,759 | 29 | 86,009 | 12 | 75,222 | 41 |
| Functional Specialist | 60,905 | 145 | 64,933 | 122 | 62,745 | 267 |
| Subject Specialist | 64,099 | 139 | 68,141 | 62 | 65,346 | 201 |
| | | | | | | |
| Dept. Head: | | | | | | |
|   Acquisitions | ‡ | 8 | ‡ | 1 | 71,058 | 9 |
|   Reference | 79,622 | 8 | . | | 79,622 | 8 |
|   Cataloging | ‡ | 19 | ‡ | 2 | 72,608 | 21 |
|   Serials | ‡ | 1 | . | | ‡ | 1 |
|   Documents/Maps | ‡ | 3 | ‡ | 1 | 66,780 | 4 |
|   Circulation | ‡ | 2 | ‡ | 4 | 72,212 | 6 |
|   Rare Books/Manuscripts | ‡ | 5 | ‡ | 1 | 77,423 | 6 |
|   Computer Systems | 85,930 | 4 | 81,717 | 8 | 83,121 | 12 |
|   Other | 76,895 | 41 | 76,174 | 19 | 76,667 | 60 |
| | | | | | | |
| Reference: | | | | | | |
|   Over 14 years experience | 69,520 | 44 | 67,587 | 16 | 69,005 | 60 |
|   10 to 14 years experience | 56,684 | 9 | 58,217 | 7 | 57,355 | 16 |
|   5 to 9 years experience | 53,539 | 30 | 57,871 | 8 | 54,451 | 38 |
|   Under 5 years experience | 47,094 | 25 | 49,822 | 6 | 47,622 | 31 |
| | | | | | | |
| Cataloging: | | | | | | |
|   Over 14 years experience | 62,452 | 39 | 71,139 | 13 | 64,624 | 52 |
|   10 to 14 years experience | 56,659 | 12 | 63,950 | 7 | 59,345 | 19 |
|   5 to 9 years experience | 52,814 | 26 | 54,487 | 4 | 53,037 | 30 |
|   Under 5 years experience | ‡ | 15 | ‡ | 3 | 50,548 | 18 |
| | | | | | | |
| Other: | | | | | | |
|   Over 14 years experience | 66,684 | 18 | 63,594 | 6 | 65,911 | 24 |
|   10 to 14 years experience | ‡ | 8 | ‡ | 2 | 53,988 | 10 |
|   5 to 9 years experience | ‡ | 16 | ‡ | 2 | 59,301 | 18 |
|   Under 5 years experience | ‡ | 20 | ‡ | 1 | 48,938 | 21 |
| | | | | | | |
| **All Positions** | **$65,372** | **694** | **$69,565** | **320** | **$66,695** | **1,014** |

Excludes Canadian libraries.
~~Excludes medical and law libraries.~~
‡ Salary data are not published when fewer than four individuals are involved in either category.
. No positions reported in this category.

## TABLE 28: NUMBER AND AVERAGE YEARS OF EXPERIENCE OF MINORITY US ARL UNIVERSITY LIBRARIANS BY POSITION AND SEX, FY 2010–2011

| Position | WOMEN | | MEN | | TOTAL | |
|---|---|---|---|---|---|---|
| | Years | No. | Years | No. | Years | No. |
| Director | 30.4 | 5 | 43.0 | 2 | 34.0 | 7 |
| Associate Director | 28.9 | 17 | 21.5 | 4 | 27.5 | 21 |
| Assistant Director | 24.7 | 6 | 16.0 | 7 | 20.0 | 13 |
| Head, Branch | 21.0 | 29 | 21.1 | 12 | 21.0 | 41 |
| Functional Specialist | 12.9 | 145 | 12.8 | 122 | 12.8 | 267 |
| Subject Specialist | 14.1 | 139 | 14.1 | 62 | 14.1 | 201 |
| | | | | | | |
| Dept. Head: | | | | | | |
| Acquisitions | 14.4 | 8 | 4.0 | 1 | 13.2 | 9 |
| Reference | 23.8 | 8 | . | | 23.8 | 8 |
| Cataloging | 20.4 | 19 | 24.5 | 2 | 20.8 | 21 |
| Serials | 19.0 | 1 | . | | 19.0 | 1 |
| Documents/Maps | 12.3 | 3 | 13.0 | 1 | 12.5 | 4 |
| Circulation | 8.5 | 2 | 22.8 | 4 | 18.0 | 6 |
| Rare Books/Manuscripts | 16.6 | 5 | 18.0 | 1 | 16.8 | 6 |
| Computer Systems | 18.8 | 4 | 14.1 | 8 | 15.7 | 12 |
| Other | 17.6 | 41 | 17.6 | 19 | 17.6 | 60 |
| | | | | | | |
| Public services | 10.7 | 32 | 13.2 | 5 | 11.0 | 37 |
| Technical services | 12.1 | 17 | . | | 12.1 | 17 |
| Administration | 13.1 | 13 | 13.8 | 6 | 13.3 | 19 |
| Reference | 13.6 | 108 | 14.5 | 37 | 13.8 | 145 |
| Cataloger | 14.7 | 92 | 17.1 | 27 | 15.2 | 119 |
| **All Positions** | **15.0** | **694** | **14.8** | **320** | **14.9** | **1,014** |

Excludes Canadian libraries. See Table 33 for comparable figures for Canadian libraries.
Excludes medical and law libraries. See Tables 40 and 47 for comparable figures for medical and law libraries.
. No positions reported in this category.

## TABLE 29: NUMBER AND AVERAGE SALARIES OF US ARL UNIVERSITY LIBRARIANS BY YEARS OF EXPERIENCE AND SEX, FY 2010–2011

| Position | WOMEN | | MEN | | TOTAL | | % OF TOTAL |
|---|---|---|---|---|---|---|---|
| | Salary | No. | Salary | No. | Salary | No. | |
| 0–3 years | $50,437 | 416 | $51,655 | 237 | $50,879 | 653 | 9% |
| 4–7 years | 53,716 | 659 | 56,196 | 372 | 54,611 | 1,031 | 14% |
| 8–11 years | 60,601 | 634 | 64,110 | 422 | 62,003 | 1,056 | 14% |
| 12–15 years | 66,239 | 571 | 69,796 | 376 | 67,651 | 947 | 13% |
| 16–19 years | 70,173 | 421 | 74,615 | 274 | 71,924 | 695 | 9% |
| 20–23 years | 74,557 | 493 | 76,089 | 288 | 75,122 | 781 | 11% |
| 24–27 years | 78,798 | 394 | 83,694 | 222 | 80,563 | 616 | 8% |
| 28–31 years | 84,307 | 364 | 85,557 | 224 | 84,783 | 588 | 8% |
| 32–35 years | 89,270 | 304 | 99,893 | 204 | 93,536 | 508 | 7% |
| over 35 years | 94,710 | 331 | 98,914 | 166 | 96,114 | 497 | 7% |
| **All Positions** | **$69,576** | **4,587** | **$73,015** | **2,785** | **$70,875** | **7,372** | **100%** |

Excludes Canadian libraries.
Excludes medical and law libraries.

## TABLE 30: NUMBER AND AVERAGE SALARIES OF MINORITY US ARL UNIVERSITY LIBRARIANS BY YEARS OF EXPERIENCE AND SEX, FY 2010–2011

| Position | WOMEN Salary | No. | MEN Salary | No. | TOTAL Salary | No. | % OF TOTAL |
|---|---|---|---|---|---|---|---|
| 0–3 years | $51,399 | 91 | $55,956 | 25 | $52,381 | 116 | 11% |
| 4–7 years | 54,481 | 131 | 56,676 | 58 | 55,155 | 189 | 19% |
| 8–11 years | 59,618 | 96 | 67,962 | 71 | 63,165 | 167 | 16% |
| 12–15 years | 66,708 | 81 | 68,946 | 52 | 67,583 | 133 | 13% |
| 16–19 years | 67,519 | 77 | 76,328 | 27 | 69,806 | 104 | 10% |
| 20-23 years | 76,128 | 76 | 74,583 | 23 | 75,769 | 99 | 10% |
| 24–27 years | 74,361 | 41 | 77,830 | 15 | 75,290 | 56 | 6% |
| 28–31 years | 73,047 | 34 | 77,017 | 21 | 74,563 | 55 | 5% |
| 32–35 years | 84,712 | 28 | 83,823 | 12 | 84,445 | 40 | 4% |
| over 35 years | 90,728 | 39 | 99,819 | 16 | 93,373 | 55 | 5% |
| **All Positions** | **$65,372** | **694** | **$69,565** | **320** | **$66,695** | **1,014** | **100%** |

Excludes Canadian libraries.
Excludes medical and law libraries.

# Canadian ARL University Libraries

## Tables 31–34

## TABLE 31: FILLED POSITIONS; AVERAGE, MEDIAN, AND BEGINNING PROFESSIONAL SALARIES; AND AVERAGE YEARS OF PROFESSIONAL EXPERIENCE IN CANADIAN ARL UNIVERSITY LIBRARIES, FY 2010–2011

| Institution | FILLED POSITIONS FY 2011 | AVERAGE SALARIES FY 2010 | AVERAGE SALARIES FY 2011 | MEDIAN SALARIES FY 2010 | MEDIAN SALARIES FY 2011 | BEGINNING SALARIES FY 2010 | BEGINNING SALARIES FY 2011 | AVERAGE YRS. EXP. FY 2011 |
|---|---|---|---|---|---|---|---|---|
| Alberta ‡ | 72 | $98,203 | $101,564 | $104,209 | $102,139 | $50,632 | $55,770 | 15.7 |
| British Columbia ‡ | 72 | 85,196 | 89,757 | 81,675 | 87,753 | 55,335 | 55,335 | 17.7 |
| Calgary ‡ | 53 | 94,823 | 96,879 | 89,543 | 93,666 | 58,000 | 58,000 | 18.7 |
| Guelph ‡ | 50 | 80,634 | 85,069 | 78,054 | 81,146 | 59,699 | 61,639 | 18.1 |
| Laval | 65 | 72,293 | 71,189 | 72,888 | 73,833 | 49,547 | 49,547 | 13.1 |
| McGill | 64 | 74,432 | 75,422 | 67,475 | 68,471 | 50,000 | 50,000 | 15.7 |
| McMaster ‡ | 45 | 71,878 | 72,880 | 72,928 | 65,572 | 46,817 | 48,500 | 17.6 |
| Manitoba ‡ | 40 | 95,500 | 96,777 | 100,070 | 100,644 | 48,820 | 48,820 | 22.9 |
| Montreal ‡ | 89 | 73,199 | 74,421 | 69,243 | 69,243 | 43,130 | 45,915 | 15.3 |
| Ottawa ‡* | 34 | N/A | 92,217 | N/A | 89,855 | N/A | 50,181 | 18.9 |
| Queen's | 32 | 93,924 | 101,504 | 97,348 | 104,510 | 51,600 | 53,251 | 21.3 |
| Saskatchewan ‡ | 46 | 89,027 | 89,895 | 91,994 | 86,118 | 52,731 | 55,104 | 16.0 |
| Toronto ‡ | 141 | 91,249 | 90,332 | 87,729 | 86,827 | 51,900 | 52,200 | 15.6 |
| Waterloo ‡ | 36 | 81,938 | 80,906 | 81,972 | 80,198 | 51,804 | 51,840 | 17.4 |
| Western Ontario ‡ | 65 | 68,921 | 72,394 | 65,014 | 70,684 | 47,380 | 50,496 | 13.4 |
| York ‡ | 53 | 96,016 | 105,317 | 90,210 | 101,808 | 49,000 | 49,000 | 17.6 |

Salaries are expressed in Canadian dollars.

Excludes Canadian medical and law libraries. See Tables 35 and 42 for comparable figures for medical and law libraries.

Directors are included in figures for average years of experience and filled positions, but not in either the average or median salary statistics.

‡ See Footnotes.

* Ottawa became a member in 2010.

## TABLE 32: NUMBER AND AVERAGE SALARIES OF CANADIAN ARL UNIVERSITY LIBRARIANS BY POSITION AND SEX, FY 2010–2011

| Position | WOMEN | | MEN | | TOTAL | |
|---|---|---|---|---|---|---|
| | Salary | No. | Salary | No. | Salary | No. |
| Director | $175,367 | 9 | $178,049 | 7 | $176,540 | 16 |
| Associate Director | 129,756 | 31 | 123,607 | 15 | 127,751 | 46 |
| Assistant Director | 106,501 | 11 | 111,356 | 6 | 108,215 | 17 |
| Head, Branch | 103,962 | 50 | 98,678 | 12 | 102,939 | 62 |
| Functional Specialist | 77,459 | 82 | 81,673 | 85 | 79,604 | 167 |
| Subject Specialist | 73,220 | 87 | 81,272 | 43 | 75,883 | 130 |
| | | | | | | |
| Dept. Head: | | | | | | |
|   Acquisitions | 93,517 | 12 | 105,718 | 4 | 96,568 | 16 |
|   Reference | ‡ | 11 | ‡ | 1 | 95,521 | 12 |
|   Cataloging | ‡ | 10 | ‡ | 2 | 97,513 | 12 |
|   Serials | 97,445 | 4 | | . | 97,445 | 4 |
|   Documents/Maps | 105,266 | 5 | 96,472 | 4 | 101,357 | 9 |
|   Circulation | ‡ | 12 | ‡ | 2 | 83,269 | 14 |
|   Rare Books/Manuscripts | ‡ | 4 | ‡ | 3 | 96,851 | 7 |
|   Computer Systems | 104,481 | 4 | 96,611 | 5 | 100,109 | 9 |
|   Other | 96,866 | 47 | 95,805 | 21 | 96,538 | 68 |
| | | | | | | |
| Reference: | | | | | | |
|   Over 14 years experience | 97,734 | 70 | 101,137 | 23 | 98,575 | 93 |
|   10 to 14 years experience | 80,562 | 24 | 78,851 | 14 | 79,932 | 38 |
|   5 to 9 years experience | 72,445 | 49 | 74,644 | 14 | 72,934 | 63 |
|   Under 5 years experience | 65,610 | 48 | 68,923 | 11 | 66,227 | 59 |
| | | | | | | |
| Cataloging: | | | | | | |
|   Over 14 years experience | 87,762 | 22 | 85,128 | 12 | 86,832 | 34 |
|   10 to 14 years experience | ‡ | 6 | ‡ | 1 | 75,420 | 7 |
|   5 to 9 years experience | 77,599 | 8 | 68,943 | 4 | 74,714 | 12 |
|   Under 5 years experience | ‡ | 6 | ‡ | 3 | 70,048 | 9 |
| | | | | | | |
| Other: | | | | | | |
|   Over 14 years experience | 86,571 | 14 | 86,691 | 6 | 86,607 | 20 |
|   10 to 14 years experience | ‡ | 10 | ‡ | 2 | 73,714 | 12 |
|   5 to 9 years experience | ‡ | 5 | ‡ | 2 | 71,862 | 7 |
|   Under 5 years experience | 63,916 | 10 | 61,856 | 4 | 63,327 | 14 |
| **All Positions** | **$87,490** | **651** | **$89,278** | **306** | **$88,062** | **957** |

Salaries are expressed in Canadian dollars.

Excludes Canadian medical and law libraries. See Tables 39 and 46 for comparable figures for medical and law libraries.

† Salary data are not published when fewer than four individuals are involved in either category.

. No positions reported in this category.

## TABLE 33: NUMBER AND AVERAGE YEARS OF EXPERIENCE OF CANADIAN ARL UNIVERSITY LIBRARIANS BY POSITION AND SEX, FY 2010–2011

| Position | WOMEN | | MEN | | TOTAL | |
|---|---|---|---|---|---|---|
| | Years | No. | Years | No. | Years | No. |
| Director | 33.6 | 9 | 31.3 | 7 | 32.6 | 16 |
| Associate Director | 24.3 | 31 | 22.3 | 15 | 23.7 | 46 |
| Assistant Director | 23.5 | 11 | 24.2 | 6 | 23.7 | 17 |
| Head, Branch | 21.1 | 50 | 19.7 | 12 | 20.8 | 62 |
| Functional Specialist | 13.4 | 82 | 15.5 | 85 | 14.5 | 167 |
| Subject Specialist | 13.4 | 87 | 14.8 | 43 | 13.9 | 130 |
| | | | | | | |
| Dept. Head: | | | | | | |
| Acquisitions | 18.1 | 12 | 22.0 | 4 | 19.1 | 16 |
| Reference | 16.8 | 11 | 32.0 | 1 | 18.1 | 12 |
| Cataloging | 25.4 | 10 | 25.5 | 2 | 25.4 | 12 |
| Serials | 22.8 | 4 | . | | 22.8 | 4 |
| Documents/Maps | 30.4 | 5 | 17.3 | 4 | 24.6 | 9 |
| Circulation | 21.3 | 12 | 6.5 | 2 | 19.1 | 14 |
| Rare Books/Manuscripts | 18.3 | 4 | 30.0 | 3 | 23.3 | 7 |
| Computer Systems | 23.3 | 4 | 16.0 | 5 | 19.2 | 9 |
| Other | 21.0 | 47 | 17.0 | 21 | 19.7 | 68 |
| | | | | | | |
| Public services | 10.3 | 12 | 7.4 | 7 | 9.2 | 19 |
| Technical services | 14.9 | 8 | 18.0 | 5 | 16.1 | 13 |
| Administration | 15.1 | 19 | 14.5 | 2 | 15.0 | 21 |
| Reference | 13.3 | 191 | 13.7 | 62 | 13.4 | 253 |
| Cataloger | 19.0 | 42 | 20.5 | 20 | 19.5 | 62 |
| | | | | | | |
| **All Positions** | **16.6** | **651** | **16.7** | **306** | **16.6** | **957** |

Excludes Canadian medical and law libraries. See Tables 40 and 47 for comparable figures for medical and law libraries.
. No positions reported in this category.

## TABLE 34: NUMBER AND AVERAGE SALARIES OF CANADIAN ARL UNIVERSITY LIBRARIANS BY YEARS OF EXPERIENCE AND SEX, FY 2010–2011

| Experience | WOMEN | | MEN | | TOTAL | | % OF TOTAL |
|---|---|---|---|---|---|---|---|
| | Salary | No. | Salary | No. | Salary | No. | |
| 0–3 years | $62,872 | 94 | $66,013 | 44 | $63,874 | 138 | 14% |
| 4–7 years | 72,092 | 95 | 73,865 | 36 | 72,579 | 131 | 14% |
| 8–11 years | 78,313 | 91 | 79,432 | 45 | 78,683 | 136 | 14% |
| 12–15 years | 87,546 | 61 | 86,036 | 29 | 87,060 | 90 | 9% |
| 16–19 years | 89,235 | 52 | 93,976 | 28 | 90,894 | 80 | 8% |
| 20–23 years | 97,164 | 67 | 94,142 | 31 | 96,208 | 98 | 10% |
| 24–27 years | 102,916 | 48 | 100,768 | 35 | 102,011 | 83 | 9% |
| 28–31 years | 106,541 | 52 | 111,132 | 21 | 107,862 | 73 | 8% |
| 32–35 years | 102,699 | 43 | 108,245 | 18 | 104,335 | 61 | 6% |
| over 35 years | 118,424 | 48 | 122,471 | 19 | 119,572 | 67 | 7% |
| **All Positions** | **$87,490** | **651** | **$89,278** | **306** | **$88,062** | **957** | **100%** |

Salaries are expressed in Canadian dollars
Excludes Canadian medical and law libraries. See Tables 41 and 48 for comparable figures for medical and law libraries.

# ARL University Medical Libraries

## Tables 35–41

## TABLE 35: FILLED POSITIONS; AVERAGE, MEDIAN, AND BEGINNING SALARIES; AND AVERAGE YEARS OF EXPERIENCE IN ARL UNIVERSITY MEDICAL LIBRARIES, FY 2010-2011

| Institution | Filled Positions | Average Salary | Median Salary | Beginning Salary | Average Yrs. Exp. |
|---|---|---|---|---|---|
| Alabama | 2 | ‡ | ‡ | $42,000 | 17.0 |
| Alberta | 6 | $87,808 | $105,587 | 52,833 | 16.7 |
| Arizona | 16 | 63,668 | 58,651 | 50,857 | 20.9 |
| Boston University | 12 | 55,599 | 50,142 | 43,000 | 8.0 |
| British Columbia | 12 | 79,772 | 82,574 | 52,420 | 18.9 |
| Calgary | 12 | 73,414 | 67,294 | 54,945 | 11.0 |
| California, Davis | 7 | 72,319 | 64,560 | 46,164 | 22.9 |
| California, Los Angeles | 11 | 82,699 | 81,876 | 46,164 | 22.5 |
| California, San Diego | 9 | 69,359 | 72,345 | 46,164 | 13.7 |
| Case Western Reserve | 7 | 67,306 | 71,055 | 35,000 | 27.9 |
| Cincinnati | 14 | 61,133 | 50,688 | 42,000 | 22.3 |
| Columbia | 10 | 70,545 | 73,803 | 52,000 | 15.7 |
| Connecticut | 15 | 77,815 | 75,152 | 55,347 | 17.5 |
| Cornell | 12 | 76,332 | 75,542 | 55,000 | 18.6 |
| Dartmouth | 8 | 63,723 | 64,415 | 45,500 | 20.8 |
| Duke | 20 | 58,074 | 55,164 | 40,000 | 16.2 |
| Emory | 12 | 62,851 | 56,959 | 47,750 | 20.4 |
| Florida | 14 | 54,305 | 48,746 | 42,000 | 13.4 |
| Florida State | 5 | 51,041 | 52,299 | 42,000 | 14.0 |
| George Washington | 14 | 66,900 | 67,542 | 42,000 | 15.6 |
| Georgetown | 12 | 60,976 | 62,500 | 44,000 | 13.1 |
| Harvard | 59 | 78,066 | 75,531 | 53,093 | 5.4 |
| Hawaii | 3 | ‡ | ‡ | 45,000 | 17.7 |
| Howard | 7 | 67,369 | 60,776 | 50,000 | 21.3 |
| Illinois, Chicago | 22 | 59,275 | 55,697 | 47,000 | 14.2 |
| Iowa | 9 | 58,790 | 52,470 | 41,000 | 16.2 |
| Johns Hopkins | 22 | 69,218 | 66,656 | 47,700 | 16.5 |
| Kansas | 11 | 50,383 | 47,370 | 43,000 | 13.3 |
| Kentucky | 14 | 56,480 | 54,282 | 41,000 | 24.1 |
| Louisiana State | 1 | ‡ | ‡ | 36,000 | 5.0 |
| Louisville | 9 | 58,207 | 56,293 | 37,000 | 24.6 |
| McGill | 10 | 72,707 | 70,071 | 47,366 | 17.8 |
| McMaster | 8 | 68,521 | 76,034 | 45,945 | 13.1 |
| Manitoba | 18 | 72,939 | 71,754 | 46,249 | 15.4 |
| Miami | 19 | 53,211 | 51,461 | 47,000 | 7.3 |
| Michigan | 19 | 60,267 | 57,296 | 42,000 | 13.5 |
| Minnesota | 15 | 63,946 | 62,846 | 43,000 | 17.1 |
| Missouri | 9 | 53,831 | 50,017 | 40,000 | 21.8 |
| Montreal | 10 | 69,345 | 65,596 | 50,297 | 16.1 |
| Nebraska | 15 | 62,725 | 57,200 | 45,000 | 19.9 |
| New Mexico | 14 | 65,631 | 62,620 | 39,372 | 21.4 |
| New York University | 35 | 67,132 | 62,700 | 50,000 | 11.9 |

## TABLE 35: FILLED POSITIONS; AVERAGE, MEDIAN, AND BEGINNING SALARIES; AND AVERAGE YEARS OF EXPERIENCE IN ARL UNIVERSITY MEDICAL LIBRARIES, FY 2010-2011

| Institution | Filled Positions | Average Salary | Median Salary | Beginning Salary | Average Yrs. Exp. |
|---|---|---|---|---|---|
| North Carolina | 30 | 68,618 | 65,049 | 45,000 | 19.8 |
| Northwestern | 17 | 65,507 | 66,073 | 41,000 | 16.9 |
| Ohio State | 11 | 62,170 | 59,919 | 43,243 | 15.9 |
| Oklahoma | 9 | 59,817 | 60,019 | 40,000 | 19.9 |
| Oklahoma State | 4 | ‡ | ‡ | 38,000 | 23.0 |
| Ottawa | 6 | 78,426 | 73,277 | 47,538 | 17.8 |
| Pennsylvania | 10 | 65,949 | 61,727 | 49,000 | 21.6 |
| Pennsylvania State | 5 | 63,993 | 62,982 | 43,709 | 17.4 |
| Pittsburgh | 25 | 62,379 | 60,227 | 45,000 | 16.2 |
| Queen's | 8 | 86,981 | 85,492 | 50,446 | 17.8 |
| Rochester | 25 | 56,577 | 53,001 | 38,983 | 20.2 |
| Saskatchewan | 6 | 72,571 | 69,604 | 52,202 | 10.3 |
| South Carolina | 9 | 49,291 | 46,692 | 35,000 | 14.3 |
| Southern California | 14 | 72,947 | 71,300 | 50,000 | 17.9 |
| Southern Illinois | 5 | 63,036 | 66,247 | 41,000 | 24.4 |
| SUNY Buffalo | 14 | 68,258 | 65,833 | 47,000 | 21.4 |
| SUNY Stony Brook | 19 | 70,087 | 71,317 | 45,000 | 15.1 |
| Temple | 9 | 57,880 | 57,680 | 44,004 | 17.8 |
| Tennessee, Knoxville | 4 | ‡ | ‡ | 40,000 | 14.0 |
| Tennessee, Memphis | 11 | 53,636 | 51,091 | 45,000 | 26.1 |
| Texas Tech | 23 | 49,315 | 45,634 | 38,110 | 19.5 |
| Toronto | 13 | 88,333 | 89,289 | 49,451 | 17.4 |
| Tulane | 14 | 40,606 | 38,684 | 40,000 | 13.0 |
| Utah | 13 | 66,845 | 60,173 | 40,000 | 22.8 |
| Vanderbilt | 13 | 63,781 | 67,060 | 41,000 | 17.3 |
| Virginia | 14 | 65,115 | 65,700 | 45,000 | 22.3 |
| Washington | 20 | 63,846 | 59,040 | 42,600 | 19.9 |
| Washington U.-St. Louis | 24 | 61,693 | 51,750 | 40,000 | 18.2 |
| Wayne State | 4 | ‡ | ‡ | 45,000 | 19.3 |
| Wisconsin | 16 | 58,988 | 56,669 | 40,526 | 13.8 |
| Yale | 20 | 76,505 | 75,556 | 50,500 | 17.6 |

Directors are included in figures for filled positions and average years of experience, but not in either the average or median salary statistics. Canadian salaries are expressed in US dollars.

‡ Salary data are not published when fewer than four individuals are involved.

## TABLE 36: BEGINNING PROFESSIONAL SALARIES IN ARL UNIVERSITY MEDICAL LIBRARIES
## RANK ORDER TABLE, FY 2010–2011

| Rank | Institution | Salary | Rank | Institution | Salary |
|------|-------------|--------|------|-------------|--------|
| 1 | Connecticut | 55,347 | 31 | Wayne State | 45,000 |
| 2 | Cornell | 55,000 | 39 | Temple | 44,004 |
| 3 | Calgary | 54,945 | 40 | Georgetown | 44,000 |
| 4 | Harvard | 53,093 | 41 | Pennsylvania State | 43,709 |
| 5 | Alberta | 52,833 | 42 | Ohio State | 43,243 |
| 6 | British Columbia | 52,420 | 43 | Boston University | 43,000 |
| 7 | Saskatchewan | 52,202 | 43 | Kansas | 43,000 |
| 8 | Columbia | 52,000 | 43 | Minnesota | 43,000 |
| 9 | Arizona | 50,857 | 46 | Washington | 42,600 |
| 10 | Yale | 50,500 | 47 | Alabama | 42,000 |
| 11 | Queen's | 50,446 | 47 | Cincinnati | 42,000 |
| 12 | Montreal | 50,297 | 47 | Florida | 42,000 |
| 13 | Howard | 50,000 | 47 | Florida State | 42,000 |
| 13 | New York University | 50,000 | 47 | George Washington | 42,000 |
| 13 | Southern California | 50,000 | 47 | Michigan | 42,000 |
| 16 | Toronto | 49,451 | 53 | Iowa | 41,000 |
| 17 | Pennsylvania | 49,000 | 53 | Kentucky | 41,000 |
| 18 | Emory | 47,750 | 53 | Northwestern | 41,000 |
| 19 | Johns Hopkins | 47,700 | 53 | Southern Illinois | 41,000 |
| 20 | Ottawa | 47,538 | 53 | Vanderbilt | 41,000 |
| 21 | McGill | 47,366 | 58 | Wisconsin | 40,526 |
| 22 | Illinois, Chicago | 47,000 | 59 | Duke | 40,000 |
| 22 | Miami | 47,000 | 59 | Missouri | 40,000 |
| 22 | SUNY Buffalo | 47,000 | 59 | Oklahoma | 40,000 |
| 25 | Manitoba | 46,249 | 59 | Tennessee, Knoxville | 40,000 |
| 26 | California, Davis | 46,164 | 59 | Tulane | 40,000 |
| 26 | California, Los Angeles | 46,164 | 59 | Utah | 40,000 |
| 26 | California, San Diego | 46,164 | 59 | Washington U.-St. Louis | 40,000 |
| 29 | McMaster | 45,945 | 66 | New Mexico | 39,372 |
| 30 | Dartmouth | 45,500 | 67 | Rochester | 38,983 |
| 31 | Hawaii | 45,000 | 68 | Texas Tech | 38,110 |
| 31 | Nebraska | 45,000 | 69 | Oklahoma State | 38,000 |
| 31 | North Carolina | 45,000 | 70 | Louisville | 37,000 |
| 31 | Pittsburgh | 45,000 | 71 | Louisiana State | 36,000 |
| 31 | SUNY Stony Brook | 45,000 | 72 | Case Western Reserve | 35,000 |
| 31 | Tennessee, Memphis | 45,000 | 72 | South Carolina | 35,000 |
| 31 | Virginia | 45,000 | | | |

Beginning salary figures represent officially designated base, not necessarily salaries of actual incumbents.
Canadian salaries are expressed in US dollars.

## TABLE 37: MEDIAN PROFESSIONAL SALARIES IN ARL UNIVERSITY MEDICAL LIBRARIES RANK ORDER TABLE, FY 2010–2011

| Rank | Institution | Salary | Rank | Institution | Salary |
|------|-------------|--------|------|-------------|--------|
| 1 | Alberta | 105,587 | 38 | Howard | 60,776 |
| 2 | Toronto | 89,289 | 39 | Pittsburgh | 60,227 |
| 3 | Queen's | 85,492 | 40 | Utah | 60,173 |
| 4 | British Columbia | 82,574 | 41 | Oklahoma | 60,019 |
| 5 | California, Los Angeles | 81,876 | 42 | Ohio State | 59,919 |
| 6 | McMaster | 76,034 | 43 | Washington | 59,040 |
| 7 | Yale | 75,556 | 44 | Arizona | 58,651 |
| 8 | Cornell | 75,542 | 45 | Temple | 57,680 |
| 9 | Harvard | 75,531 | 46 | Michigan | 57,296 |
| 10 | Connecticut | 75,152 | 47 | Nebraska | 57,200 |
| 11 | Columbia | 73,803 | 48 | Emory | 56,959 |
| 12 | Ottawa | 73,277 | 49 | Wisconsin | 56,669 |
| 13 | California, San Diego | 72,345 | 50 | Louisville | 56,293 |
| 14 | Manitoba | 71,754 | 51 | Illinois, Chicago | 55,697 |
| 15 | SUNY Stony Brook | 71,317 | 52 | Duke | 55,164 |
| 16 | Southern California | 71,300 | 53 | Kentucky | 54,282 |
| 17 | Case Western Reserve | 71,055 | 54 | Rochester | 53,001 |
| 18 | McGill | 70,071 | 55 | Iowa | 52,470 |
| 19 | Saskatchewan | 69,604 | 56 | Florida State | 52,299 |
| 20 | George Washington | 67,542 | 57 | Washington U.-St. Louis | 51,750 |
| 21 | Calgary | 67,294 | 58 | Miami | 51,461 |
| 22 | Vanderbilt | 67,060 | 59 | Tennessee, Memphis | 51,091 |
| 23 | Johns Hopkins | 66,656 | 60 | Cincinnati | 50,688 |
| 24 | Southern Illinois | 66,247 | 61 | Boston University | 50,142 |
| 25 | Northwestern | 66,073 | 62 | Missouri | 50,017 |
| 26 | SUNY Buffalo | 65,833 | 63 | Florida | 48,746 |
| 27 | Virginia | 65,700 | 64 | Kansas | 47,370 |
| 28 | Montreal | 65,596 | 65 | South Carolina | 46,692 |
| 29 | North Carolina | 65,049 | 66 | Texas Tech | 45,634 |
| 30 | California, Davis | 64,560 | 67 | Tulane | 38,684 |
| 31 | Dartmouth | 64,415 | | Alabama | * |
| 32 | Pennsylvania State | 62,982 | | Hawaii | * |
| 33 | Minnesota | 62,846 | | Louisiana State | * |
| 34 | New York University | 62,700 | | Oklahoma State | * |
| 35 | New Mexico | 62,620 | | Tennessee, Knoxville | * |
| 36 | Georgetown | 62,500 | | Wayne State | * |
| 37 | Pennsylvania | 61,727 | | | |

Salaries of directors are not included in the calculation of medians.

Alabama, Hawaii, Louisiana State, Oklahoma State, Tennessee-Knoxville, and Wayne State, are not ranked because they reported four or fewer individuals.

Canadian salaries are expressed in US dollars.

## TABLE 38: AVERAGE PROFESSIONAL SALARIES IN ARL UNIVERSITY MEDICAL LIBRARIES
## RANK ORDER TABLE, FY 2010–2011

| Rank | Institution | Salary | Rank | Institution | Salary |
|------|-------------|--------|------|-------------|--------|
| 1 | Toronto | 88,333 | 38 | Dartmouth | 63,723 |
| 2 | Alberta | 87,808 | 39 | Arizona | 63,668 |
| 3 | Queen's | 86,981 | 40 | Southern Illinois | 63,036 |
| 4 | California, Los Angeles | 82,699 | 41 | Emory | 62,851 |
| 5 | British Columbia | 79,772 | 42 | Nebraska | 62,725 |
| 6 | Ottawa | 78,426 | 43 | Pittsburgh | 62,379 |
| 7 | Harvard | 78,066 | 44 | Ohio State | 62,170 |
| 8 | Connecticut | 77,815 | 45 | Washington U.-St. Louis | 61,693 |
| 9 | Yale | 76,505 | 46 | Cincinnati | 61,133 |
| 10 | Cornell | 76,332 | 47 | Georgetown | 60,976 |
| 11 | Calgary | 73,414 | 48 | Michigan | 60,267 |
| 12 | Southern California | 72,947 | 49 | Oklahoma | 59,817 |
| 13 | Manitoba | 72,939 | 50 | Illinois, Chicago | 59,275 |
| 14 | McGill | 72,707 | 51 | Wisconsin | 58,988 |
| 15 | Saskatchewan | 72,571 | 52 | Iowa | 58,790 |
| 16 | California, Davis | 72,319 | 53 | Louisville | 58,207 |
| 17 | Columbia | 70,545 | 54 | Duke | 58,074 |
| 18 | SUNY Stony Brook | 70,087 | 55 | Temple | 57,880 |
| 19 | California, San Diego | 69,359 | 56 | Rochester | 56,577 |
| 20 | Montreal | 69,345 | 57 | Kentucky | 56,480 |
| 21 | Johns Hopkins | 69,218 | 58 | Boston University | 55,599 |
| 22 | North Carolina | 68,618 | 59 | Florida | 54,305 |
| 23 | McMaster | 68,521 | 60 | Missouri | 53,831 |
| 24 | SUNY Buffalo | 68,258 | 61 | Tennessee, Memphis | 53,636 |
| 25 | Howard | 67,369 | 62 | Miami | 53,211 |
| 26 | Case Western Reserve | 67,306 | 63 | Florida State | 51,041 |
| 27 | New York University | 67,132 | 64 | Kansas | 50,383 |
| 28 | George Washington | 66,900 | 65 | Texas Tech | 49,315 |
| 29 | Utah | 66,845 | 66 | South Carolina | 49,291 |
| 30 | Pennsylvania | 65,949 | 67 | Tulane | 40,606 |
| 31 | New Mexico | 65,631 | | Alabama | * |
| 32 | Northwestern | 65,507 | | Hawaii | * |
| 33 | Virginia | 65,115 | | Louisiana State | * |
| 34 | Pennsylvania State | 63,993 | | Oklahoma State | * |
| 35 | Minnesota | 63,946 | | Tennessee, Knoxville | * |
| 36 | Washington | 63,846 | | Wayne State | * |
| 37 | Vanderbilt | 63,781 | | | |

Salaries of directors are not included in the calculation of medians.

Alabama, Hawaii, Louisiana State, Oklahoma State, Tennessee-Knoxville, and Wayne State are not ranked because they reported four or fewer individuals.

Canadian salaries are expressed in US dollars.

## TABLE 39: NUMBER AND AVERAGE SALARIES OF ARL UNIVERSITY MEDICAL LIBRARIANS BY POSITION AND SEX, FY 2010–2011

| Position | WOMEN Salary | No. | MEN Salary | No. | TOTAL Salary | No. |
|---|---|---|---|---|---|---|
| Head, Medical | $126,693 | 52 | $131,879 | 16 | $127,913 | 68 |
| Associate Director | 84,544 | 37 | 96,530 | 15 | 88,002 | 52 |
| Assistant Director | 68,005 | 35 | 75,635 | 7 | 69,276 | 42 |
| Head, Branch | ‡ | 21 | ‡ | 1 | 68,371 | 22 |
| Functional Specialist | 62,861 | 90 | 64,613 | 94 | 63,756 | 184 |
| Subject Specialist | 63,429 | 62 | 59,891 | 11 | 62,896 | 73 |
| | | | | | | |
| Dept. Head: | | | | | | |
| Acquisitions | 65,136 | 16 | 63,049 | 6 | 64,567 | 22 |
| Reference | 68,649 | 21 | 79,757 | 6 | 71,117 | 27 |
| Cataloging | ‡ | 12 | ‡ | 2 | 69,295 | 14 |
| Serials | ‡ | 6 | ‡ | 2 | 58,744 | 8 |
| Documents/Maps | ‡ | 2 | . | | ‡ | 2 |
| Circulation | 61,362 | 11 | 63,694 | 8 | 62,344 | 19 |
| Rare Books/Manuscripts | ‡ | 2 | ‡ | 3 | 62,500 | 5 |
| Computer Systems | 82,733 | 4 | 81,916 | 8 | 82,189 | 12 |
| Other | 67,568 | 47 | 67,863 | 13 | 67,632 | 60 |
| | | | | | | |
| Reference: | | | | | | |
| Over 14 years experience | 69,080 | 93 | 70,633 | 24 | 69,398 | 117 |
| 10 to 14 years experience | 63,374 | 29 | 69,088 | 8 | 64,609 | 37 |
| 5 to 9 years experience | 60,213 | 38 | 53,954 | 8 | 59,125 | 46 |
| Under 5 years experience | 50,747 | 35 | 49,087 | 7 | 50,470 | 42 |
| | | | | | | |
| Cataloging: | | | | | | |
| Over 14 years experience | ‡ | 4 | ‡ | 2 | 67,224 | 6 |
| 10 to 14 years experience | ‡ | 3 | . | | ‡ | 3 |
| 5 to 9 years experience | 48,427 | 4 | . | | 48,427 | 4 |
| Under 5 years experience | 51,050 | 5 | . | | 51,050 | 5 |
| | | | | | | |
| Other: | | | | | | |
| Over 14 years experience | 64,245 | 30 | 64,291 | 10 | 64,256 | 40 |
| 10 to 14 years experience | ‡ | 12 | ‡ | 2 | 56,317 | 14 |
| 5 to 9 years experience | 55,550 | 18 | 57,587 | 6 | 56,059 | 24 |
| Under 5 years experience | 46,035 | 18 | 54,009 | 8 | 48,489 | 26 |
| | | | | | | |
| **All Positions** | **$69,092** | **707** | **$70,912** | **267** | **$69,591** | **974** |

Canadian salaries are expressed in US dollars.

‡ Salary data are not published when fewer than four individuals are involved in either category.

. No positions reported in this category.

## TABLE 40: NUMBER AND AVERAGE YEARS OF EXPERIENCE OF ARL UNIVERSITY MEDICAL LIBRARIANS BY POSITION AND SEX, FY 2010–2011

| Position | WOMEN | | MEN | | TOTAL | |
|---|---|---|---|---|---|---|
| | Years | No. | Years | No. | Years | No. |
| Head, Medical | 30.3 | 52 | 29.5 | 16 | 30.1 | 68 |
| Associate Director | 22.6 | 37 | 26.1 | 15 | 23.6 | 52 |
| Assistant Director | 20.8 | 35 | 16.4 | 7 | 20.1 | 42 |
| Head, Branch | 19.6 | 21 | 8.0 | 1 | 19.1 | 22 |
| Functional Specialist | 12.7 | 90 | 10.1 | 94 | 11.3 | 184 |
| Subject Specialist | 16.6 | 62 | 12.5 | 11 | 16.0 | 73 |
| | | | | | | |
| Dept. Head: | | | | | | |
|   Acquisitions | 18.6 | 16 | 15.2 | 6 | 17.6 | 22 |
|   Reference | 20.8 | 21 | 23.2 | 6 | 21.3 | 27 |
|   Cataloging | 20.3 | 12 | 22.0 | 2 | 20.6 | 14 |
|   Serials | 17.0 | 6 | 15.5 | 2 | 16.6 | 8 |
|   Documents/Maps | 10.5 | 2 | . | | 10.5 | 2 |
|   Circulation | 20.1 | 11 | 9.6 | 8 | 15.7 | 19 |
|   Rare Books/Manuscripts | 21.0 | 2 | 25.3 | 3 | 23.6 | 5 |
|   Computer Systems | 18.8 | 4 | 18.8 | 8 | 18.8 | 12 |
|   Other | 17.1 | 47 | 14.9 | 13 | 16.7 | 60 |
| | | | | | | |
| Public services | 13.6 | 53 | 9.3 | 15 | 12.6 | 68 |
| Technical services | 13.2 | 13 | 18.8 | 6 | 15.0 | 19 |
| Administration | 14.3 | 12 | 15.2 | 5 | 14.6 | 17 |
| Reference | 15.7 | 195 | 15.4 | 47 | 15.6 | 242 |
| Cataloger | 9.8 | 16 | 27.0 | 2 | 11.7 | 18 |
| **All Positions** | **17.3** | **707** | **14.9** | **267** | **16.7** | **974** |

. No positions were reported in this category.

## Table 41: Number and Average Salaries of ARL University Medical Librarians by Years of Experience and Sex, FY 2010–2011

| Experience | WOMEN | | MEN | | TOTAL | | % OF TOTAL |
|---|---|---|---|---|---|---|---|
| | Salary | No. | Salary | No. | Salary | No. | |
| 0–3 years | $55,288 | 85 | $57,331 | 53 | $56,073 | 138 | 14% |
| 4–7 years | 55,633 | 102 | 56,790 | 34 | 55,922 | 136 | 14% |
| 8–11 years | 61,589 | 94 | 69,070 | 41 | 63,861 | 135 | 14% |
| 12–15 years | 68,313 | 68 | 69,408 | 24 | 68,599 | 92 | 9% |
| 16–19 years | 68,195 | 68 | 73,987 | 28 | 69,884 | 96 | 10% |
| 20–23 years | 70,567 | 51 | 80,979 | 17 | 73,170 | 68 | 7% |
| 24–27 years | 74,598 | 63 | 90,468 | 17 | 77,970 | 80 | 8% |
| 28–31 years | 79,810 | 71 | 78,316 | 22 | 79,457 | 93 | 10% |
| 32–35 years | 86,855 | 56 | 79,489 | 21 | 84,846 | 77 | 8% |
| over 35 years | 93,326 | 49 | 108,785 | 10 | 95,946 | 59 | 6% |
| **All Positions** | **$69,092** | **707** | **$70,912** | **267** | **$69,591** | **974** | **100%** |

Canadian salaries are expressed in US dollars.

# ARL University Law Libraries

## Tables 42–48

## TABLE 42: FILLED POSITIONS; AVERAGE, MEDIAN, AND BEGINNING SALARIES; AND AVERAGE YEARS OF EXPERIENCE IN ARL UNIVERSITY LAW LIBRARIES, FY 2010–2011

| Institution | Filled Positions | Average Salary | Median Salary | Beginning Salary | Average Yrs. Exp. |
|---|---|---|---|---|---|
| Alberta | 4 | ‡ | ‡ | $52,833 | 29.5 |
| Arizona | 8 | $64,267 | $65,341 | 50,000 | 18.3 |
| Arizona State | 6 | 68,202 | 73,168 | 46,500 | 25.7 |
| Boston University | 11 | 74,520 | 69,700 | 55,000 | 17.8 |
| Boston College | 16 | 68,694 | 67,000 | 43,350 | 18.2 |
| British Columbia | 3 | ‡ | ‡ | 52,420 | 23.7 |
| Calgary | 3 | ‡ | ‡ | 54,945 | 19.0 |
| California, Davis | 8 | 74,131 | 68,892 | 46,164 | 18.9 |
| California, Irvine | 6 | 85,995 | 82,524 | 46,144 | 11.5 |
| California, Los Angeles | 16 | 77,676 | 82,524 | 46,164 | 14.6 |
| Case Western Reserve | 12 | 69,200 | 67,467 | 35,000 | 20.3 |
| Cincinnati | 8 | 64,512 | 54,384 | 50,000 | 19.5 |
| Colorado | 8 | 72,314 | 59,901 | 45,000 | 19.0 |
| Columbia | 17 | 78,515 | 72,891 | 52,000 | 14.0 |
| Connecticut | 9 | 72,135 | 72,097 | 50,000 | 21.8 |
| Cornell | 8 | 78,587 | 72,828 | 59,200 | 14.6 |
| Duke | 11 | 69,175 | 63,750 | 60,000 | 16.9 |
| Emory | 9 | 59,559 | 56,842 | 42,000 | 12.6 |
| Florida | 8 | 58,379 | 53,162 | 50,000 | 11.1 |
| Florida State | 9 | 54,208 | 54,815 | 50,000 | 19.6 |
| George Washington | 21 | 89,173 | 82,890 | 58,000 | 15.3 |
| Georgetown | 25 | 77,644 | 71,710 | 54,000 | 12.4 |
| Georgia | 8 | 56,405 | 55,752 | 50,000 | 14.0 |
| Harvard | 37 | 81,584 | 77,988 | 53,093 | 14.5 |
| Hawaii | 5 | 84,551 | 81,193 | 45,000 | 15.6 |
| Houston | 12 | 57,094 | 52,788 | 51,000 | 16.3 |
| Howard | 6 | 48,423 | 49,914 | 51,000 | 21.5 |
| Illinois, Urbana | 9 | 64,664 | 67,246 | 53,500 | 16.8 |
| Indiana | 10 | 69,325 | 64,923 | 40,400 | 22.0 |
| Iowa | 17 | 73,788 | 73,250 | 41,000 | 19.4 |
| Kansas | 7 | 47,022 | 44,926 | 42,000 | 9.3 |
| Kentucky | 5 | 57,520 | 52,000 | 50,000 | 13.8 |
| Louisiana State | 9 | 57,380 | 55,846 | 50,000 | 18.2 |
| Louisville | 6 | 60,053 | 59,931 | 37,000 | 20.3 |
| McGill | 5 | 83,096 | 76,437 | 47,366 | 19.6 |
| Manitoba | 3 | ‡ | ‡ | 46,249 | 29.3 |
| Miami | 13 | 60,319 | 57,688 | 45,000 | 15.7 |
| Michigan | 11 | 83,231 | 81,014 | 49,000 | 15.4 |
| Minnesota | 14 | 75,686 | 68,200 | 46,000 | 20.4 |
| Missouri | 8 | 55,073 | 57,327 | 40,000 | 14.6 |
| Montreal | 4 | ‡ | ‡ | 50,297 | 8.0 |
| Nebraska | 5 | 63,975 | 63,772 | 45,000 | 18.4 |

# TABLE 42: FILLED POSITIONS; AVERAGE, MEDIAN, AND BEGINNING SALARIES; AND AVERAGE YEARS OF EXPERIENCE IN ARL UNIVERSITY LAW LIBRARIES, FY 2010–2011

| Institution | Filled Positions | Average Salary | Median Salary | Beginning Salary | Average Yrs. Exp. |
|---|---|---|---|---|---|
| New Mexico | 8 | 64,782 | 59,760 | 50,000 | 12.8 |
| New York University | 19 | 80,014 | 76,203 | 60,000 | 22.6 |
| North Carolina | 12 | 74,737 | 68,000 | 55,000 | 16.1 |
| Northwestern | 10 | 65,860 | 61,503 | 44,000 | 22.3 |
| Notre Dame | 14 | 70,802 | 66,500 | 44,000 | 18.1 |
| Ohio State | 6 | 68,061 | 61,510 | 46,000 | 12.5 |
| Oklahoma | 7 | 57,410 | 51,269 | 45,000 | 15.7 |
| Oregon | 6 | 53,544 | 57,846 | 42,000 | 17.5 |
| Ottawa | 4 | ‡ | ‡ | 47,538 | 18.8 |
| Pennsylvania | 12 | 67,497 | 65,462 | 49,000 | 13.3 |
| Pennsylvania State | 9 | 79,637 | 73,992 | 57,000 | 23.0 |
| Queen's | 3 | ‡ | ‡ | 50,446 | 10.7 |
| Rutgers, Camden | 8 | 75,469 | 87,500 | 62,000 | 22.8 |
| Rutgers, Newark | 10 | 73,957 | 65,760 | 62,000 | 17.5 |
| Saskatchewan | 3 | ‡ | ‡ | 52,202 | 23.0 |
| South Carolina | 11 | 65,437 | 68,375 | 50,000 | 12.7 |
| Southern Illinois | 4 | ‡ | ‡ | 50,000 | 7.0 |
| SUNY Buffalo | 11 | 74,077 | 74,004 | 55,000 | 14.0 |
| Syracuse | 10 | 57,621 | 54,630 | 46,700 | 14.5 |
| Temple | 10 | 63,848 | 53,203 | 44,004 | 24.1 |
| Tennessee | 7 | 65,954 | 62,718 | 48,000 | 15.7 |
| Texas | 15 | 59,425 | 53,429 | 40,000 | 16.1 |
| Texas Tech | 8 | 60,612 | 56,990 | 47,000 | 12.8 |
| Toronto | 6 | 83,988 | 81,765 | 49,451 | 14.8 |
| Tulane | 6 | 61,297 | 59,455 | 40,000 | 19.3 |
| Utah | 8 | 57,095 | 52,530 | 41,500 | 17.5 |
| Vanderbilt | 5 | 70,083 | 61,524 | 41,000 | 21.0 |
| Virginia | 14 | 68,562 | 63,500 | 63,500 | 16.1 |
| Washington | 16 | 72,458 | 65,735 | 60,000 | 22.8 |
| Washington U.-St. Louis | 10 | 63,709 | 58,560 | 48,000 | 19.9 |
| Wayne State | 4 | ‡ | ‡ | 45,000 | 24.0 |
| Western Ontario | 3 | ‡ | ‡ | 47,836 | 15.3 |
| Wisconsin | 12 | 64,416 | 58,954 | 40,526 | 24.1 |
| Yale | 18 | 85,403 | 85,911 | 50,500 | 20.1 |
| York | 5 | 87,978 | 90,448 | 49,000 | 16.2 |

Directors are included in figures for filled positions and average years of experience, but not in either the average or median salary statistics. Canadian salaries are expressed in US dollars.

‡ Salary data are not published when fewer than four individuals are involved.

## Table 43: Beginning Professional Salaries in ARL University Law Libraries
## Rank Order Table, FY 2010–2011

| Rank | Institution | Salary | Rank | Institution | Salary |
|------|-------------|--------|------|-------------|--------|
| 1 | Virginia | 63,500 | 38 | York | 49,000 |
| 2 | Rutgers, Camden | 62,000 | 41 | Tennessee | 48,000 |
| 2 | Rutgers, Newark | 62,000 | 41 | Washington U.-St. Louis | 48,000 |
| 4 | Duke | 60,000 | 43 | Western Ontario | 47,836 |
| 4 | New York University | 60,000 | 44 | Ottawa | 47,538 |
| 4 | Washington | 60,000 | 45 | McGill | 47,366 |
| 7 | Cornell | 59,200 | 46 | Texas Tech | 47,000 |
| 8 | George Washington | 58,000 | 47 | Syracuse | 46,700 |
| 9 | Pennsylvania State | 57,000 | 48 | Arizona State | 46,500 |
| 10 | Boston University | 55,000 | 49 | Manitoba | 46,249 |
| 10 | North Carolina | 55,000 | 50 | California, Davis | 46,164 |
| 10 | SUNY Buffalo | 55,000 | 50 | California, Los Angeles | 46,164 |
| 13 | Calgary | 54,945 | 52 | California, Irvine | 46,144 |
| 14 | Georgetown | 54,000 | 53 | Minnesota | 46,000 |
| 15 | Illinois, Urbana | 53,500 | 53 | Ohio State | 46,000 |
| 16 | Harvard | 53,093 | 55 | Colorado | 45,000 |
| 17 | Alberta | 52,833 | 55 | Hawaii | 45,000 |
| 18 | British Columbia | 52,420 | 55 | Miami | 45,000 |
| 19 | Saskatchewan | 52,202 | 55 | Nebraska | 45,000 |
| 20 | Columbia | 52,000 | 55 | Oklahoma | 45,000 |
| 21 | Houston | 51,000 | 55 | Wayne State | 45,000 |
| 21 | Howard | 51,000 | 61 | Temple | 44,004 |
| 23 | Yale | 50,500 | 62 | Northwestern | 44,000 |
| 24 | Queen's | 50,446 | 62 | Notre Dame | 44,000 |
| 25 | Montreal | 50,297 | 64 | Boston College | 43,350 |
| 26 | Arizona | 50,000 | 65 | Emory | 42,000 |
| 26 | Cincinnati | 50,000 | 65 | Kansas | 42,000 |
| 26 | Connecticut | 50,000 | 65 | Oregon | 42,000 |
| 26 | Florida | 50,000 | 68 | Utah | 41,500 |
| 26 | Florida State | 50,000 | 69 | Iowa | 41,000 |
| 26 | Georgia | 50,000 | 69 | Vanderbilt | 41,000 |
| 26 | Kentucky | 50,000 | 71 | Wisconsin | 40,526 |
| 26 | Louisiana State | 50,000 | 72 | Indiana | 40,400 |
| 26 | New Mexico | 50,000 | 73 | Missouri | 40,000 |
| 26 | South Carolina | 50,000 | 73 | Texas | 40,000 |
| 26 | Southern Illinois | 50,000 | 73 | Tulane | 40,000 |
| 37 | Toronto | 49,451 | 76 | Louisville | 37,000 |
| 38 | Michigan | 49,000 | 77 | Case Western Reserve | 35,000 |
| 38 | Pennsylvania | 49,000 | | | |

Beginning salary figures represent officially designated base, not necessarily salaries of actual incumbents.
Canadian salaries are expressed in US dollars.

## Table 44: Median Professional Salaries in ARL University Law Libraries
## Rank Order Table, FY 2010–2011

| Rank | Institution | Salary | Rank | Institution | Salary |
|------|-------------|--------|------|-------------|--------|
| 1 | York | 90,448 | 40 | Ohio State | 61,510 |
| 2 | Rutgers, Camden | 87,500 | 41 | Northwestern | 61,503 |
| 3 | Yale | 85,911 | 42 | Louisville | 59,931 |
| 4 | George Washington | 82,890 | 43 | Colorado | 59,901 |
| 5 | California, Irvine | 82,524 | 44 | New Mexico | 59,760 |
| 5 | California, Los Angeles | 82,524 | 45 | Tulane | 59,455 |
| 7 | Toronto | 81,765 | 46 | Wisconsin | 58,954 |
| 8 | Hawaii | 81,193 | 47 | Washington U.-St. Louis | 58,560 |
| 9 | Michigan | 81,014 | 48 | Oregon | 57,846 |
| 10 | Harvard | 77,988 | 49 | Miami | 57,688 |
| 11 | McGill | 76,437 | 50 | Missouri | 57,327 |
| 12 | New York University | 76,203 | 51 | Texas Tech | 56,990 |
| 13 | SUNY Buffalo | 74,004 | 52 | Emory | 56,842 |
| 14 | Pennsylvania State | 73,992 | 53 | Louisiana State | 55,846 |
| 15 | Iowa | 73,250 | 54 | Georgia | 55,752 |
| 16 | Arizona State | 73,168 | 55 | Florida State | 54,815 |
| 17 | Columbia | 72,891 | 56 | Syracuse | 54,630 |
| 18 | Cornell | 72,828 | 57 | Cincinnati | 54,384 |
| 19 | Connecticut | 72,097 | 58 | Texas | 53,429 |
| 20 | Georgetown | 71,710 | 59 | Temple | 53,203 |
| 21 | Boston University | 69,700 | 60 | Florida | 53,162 |
| 22 | California, Davis | 68,892 | 61 | Houston | 52,788 |
| 23 | South Carolina | 68,375 | 62 | Utah | 52,530 |
| 24 | Minnesota | 68,200 | 63 | Kentucky | 52,000 |
| 25 | North Carolina | 68,000 | 64 | Oklahoma | 51,269 |
| 26 | Case Western Reserve | 67,467 | 65 | Howard | 49,914 |
| 27 | Illinois, Urbana | 67,246 | 66 | Kansas | 44,926 |
| 28 | Boston College | 67,000 | | Alberta | * |
| 29 | Notre Dame | 66,500 | | British Columbia | * |
| 30 | Rutgers, Newark | 65,760 | | Calgary | * |
| 31 | Washington | 65,735 | | Manitoba | * |
| 32 | Pennsylvania | 65,462 | | Montreal | * |
| 33 | Arizona | 65,341 | | Ottawa | * |
| 34 | Indiana | 64,923 | | Queen's | * |
| 35 | Nebraska | 63,772 | | Saskatchewan | * |
| 36 | Duke | 63,750 | | Southern Illinois | * |
| 37 | Virginia | 63,500 | | Wayne State | * |
| 38 | Tennessee | 62,718 | | Western Ontario | * |
| 39 | Vanderbilt | 61,524 | | | |

Salaries of directors are not included in the calculation of medians.

Alberta, British Columbia, Calgary, Manitoba, Montreal, Ottawa, Queen's, Saskatchewan, Southern Illinois, Wayne State, and Western Ontario are not ranked because they reported four or fewer individuals.

Canadian salaries are expressed in US dollars.

## TABLE 45: AVERAGE PROFESSIONAL SALARIES IN ARL UNIVERSITY LAW LIBRARIES RANK ORDER TABLE, FY 2010–2011

| Rank | Institution | Salary | Rank | Institution | Salary |
|------|-------------|--------|------|-------------|--------|
| 1 | George Washington | 89,173 | 40 | New Mexico | 64,782 |
| 2 | York | 87,978 | 41 | Illinois, Urbana | 64,664 |
| 3 | California, Irvine | 85,995 | 42 | Cincinnati | 64,512 |
| 4 | Yale | 85,403 | 43 | Wisconsin | 64,416 |
| 5 | Hawaii | 84,551 | 44 | Arizona | 64,267 |
| 6 | Toronto | 83,988 | 45 | Nebraska | 63,975 |
| 7 | Michigan | 83,231 | 46 | Temple | 63,848 |
| 8 | McGill | 83,096 | 47 | Washington U.-St. Louis | 63,709 |
| 9 | Harvard | 81,584 | 48 | Tulane | 61,297 |
| 10 | New York University | 80,014 | 49 | Texas Tech | 60,612 |
| 11 | Pennsylvania State | 79,637 | 50 | Miami | 60,319 |
| 12 | Cornell | 78,587 | 51 | Louisville | 60,053 |
| 13 | Columbia | 78,515 | 52 | Emory | 59,559 |
| 14 | California, Los Angeles | 77,676 | 53 | Texas | 59,425 |
| 15 | Georgetown | 77,644 | 54 | Florida | 58,379 |
| 16 | Minnesota | 75,686 | 55 | Syracuse | 57,621 |
| 17 | Rutgers, Camden | 75,469 | 56 | Kentucky | 57,520 |
| 18 | North Carolina | 74,737 | 57 | Oklahoma | 57,410 |
| 19 | Boston University | 74,520 | 58 | Louisiana State | 57,380 |
| 20 | California, Davis | 74,131 | 59 | Utah | 57,095 |
| 21 | SUNY Buffalo | 74,077 | 60 | Houston | 57,094 |
| 22 | Rutgers, Newark | 73,957 | 61 | Georgia | 56,405 |
| 23 | Iowa | 73,788 | 62 | Missouri | 55,073 |
| 24 | Washington | 72,458 | 63 | Florida State | 54,208 |
| 25 | Colorado | 72,314 | 64 | Oregon | 53,544 |
| 26 | Connecticut | 72,135 | 65 | Howard | 48,423 |
| 27 | Notre Dame | 70,802 | 66 | Kansas | 47,022 |
| 28 | Vanderbilt | 70,083 | | Alberta | * |
| 29 | Indiana | 69,325 | | British Columbia | * |
| 30 | Case Western Reserve | 69,200 | | Calgary | * |
| 31 | Duke | 69,175 | | Manitoba | * |
| 32 | Boston College | 68,694 | | Montreal | * |
| 33 | Virginia | 68,562 | | Ottawa | * |
| 34 | Arizona State | 68,202 | | Queen's | * |
| 35 | Ohio State | 68,061 | | Saskatchewan | * |
| 36 | Pennsylvania | 67,497 | | Southern Illinois | * |
| 37 | Tennessee | 65,954 | | Wayne State | * |
| 38 | Northwestern | 65,860 | | Western Ontario | * |
| 39 | South Carolina | 65,437 | | | |

Salaries of directors are not included in the calculation of medians.
Alberta, British Columbia, Calgary, Manitoba, Montreal, Ottawa, Queen's, Saskatchewan, Southern Illinois, Wayne State, and Western Ontario are not ranked because they reported four or fewer individuals.
Canadian salaries are expressed in US dollars.

## TABLE 46: NUMBER AND AVERAGE SALARIES OF ARL UNIVERSITY LAW LIBRARIANS BY POSITION AND SEX, FY 2010–2011

| | WOMEN | | MEN | | TOTAL | |
|---|---|---|---|---|---|---|
| **Position** | **Salary** | **No.** | **Salary** | **No.** | **Salary** | **No.** |
| Head, Law | $156,041 | 37 | $150,636 | 35 | $153,414 | 72 |
| Associate Director | 96,343 | 35 | 98,129 | 21 | 97,013 | 56 |
| Assistant Director | 88,203 | 29 | 88,835 | 12 | 88,388 | 41 |
| Functional Specialist | 61,267 | 26 | 66,671 | 28 | 64,069 | 54 |
| Subject Specialist | 73,005 | 30 | 81,425 | 10 | 75,110 | 40 |
| | | | | | | |
| Dept. Head: | | | | | | |
| Acquisitions | 66,681 | 27 | 59,784 | 8 | 65,105 | 35 |
| Reference | 77,529 | 18 | 78,105 | 6 | 77,673 | 24 |
| Cataloging | 70,736 | 26 | 65,520 | 4 | 70,040 | 30 |
| Serials | ‡ | 5 | ‡ | 1 | 69,298 | 6 |
| Documents/Maps | ‡ | 7 | ‡ | 1 | 67,239 | 8 |
| Circulation | 64,483 | 17 | 57,528 | 6 | 62,668 | 23 |
| Rare Books/Manuscripts | ‡ | 3 | . | | ‡ | 3 |
| Computer Systems | ‡ | 2 | ‡ | 6 | 83,753 | 8 |
| Other | 75,660 | 23 | 73,210 | 9 | 74,971 | 32 |
| | | | | | | |
| Reference: | | | | | | |
| Over 14 years experience | 74,618 | 47 | 74,788 | 21 | 74,671 | 68 |
| 10 to 14 years experience | 57,743 | 11 | 61,892 | 10 | 59,719 | 21 |
| 5 to 9 years experience | 63,694 | 37 | 64,895 | 21 | 64,129 | 58 |
| Under 5 years experience | 59,321 | 43 | 56,980 | 26 | 58,439 | 69 |
| | | | | | | |
| Cataloging | | | | | | |
| Over 14 years experience | 63,562 | 20 | 72,179 | 5 | 65,285 | 25 |
| 10 to 14 years experience | ‡ | 4 | ‡ | 1 | 57,455 | 5 |
| 5 to 9 years experience | 56,873 | 7 | . | | 56,873 | 7 |
| Under 5 years experience | ‡ | 2 | ‡ | 3 | 60,498 | 5 |
| | | | | | | |
| Other: | | | | | | |
| Over 14 years experience | 70,234 | 12 | 65,599 | 5 | 68,871 | 17 |
| 10 to 14 years experience | ‡ | 3 | ‡ | 1 | ‡ | 4 |
| 5 to 9 years experience | 49,333 | 4 | 72,482 | 4 | 60,907 | 8 |
| Under 5 years experience | ‡ | 13 | ‡ | 2 | 54,461 | 15 |
| | | | | | | |
| **All Positions** | **$77,036** | **488** | **$82,751** | **246** | **$78,951** | **734** |

Canadian salaries are expressed in US dollars.
‡ Salary data are not published when fewer than four individuals are involved in either category.
. No positions were reported in this category.

## Table 47: Number and Average Years of Experience of ARL University Law Librarians by Position And Sex, FY 2010–2011

| Position | Women | | Men | | Total | |
|---|---|---|---|---|---|---|
| | Years | No. | Years | No. | Years | No. |
| Head, Law | 29.5 | 37 | 23.1 | 35 | 26.3 | 72 |
| Associate Director | 24.8 | 35 | 19.5 | 21 | 22.8 | 56 |
| Assistant Director | 20.4 | 29 | 24.5 | 12 | 21.6 | 41 |
| Functional Specialist | 12.7 | 26 | 10.5 | 28 | 11.5 | 54 |
| Subject Specialist | 17.8 | 30 | 21.8 | 10 | 18.8 | 40 |
| | | | | | | |
| Dept. Head: | | | | | | |
| Acquisitions | 23.0 | 27 | 13.5 | 8 | 20.8 | 35 |
| Reference | 16.9 | 18 | 21.5 | 6 | 18.0 | 24 |
| Cataloging | 26.2 | 26 | 22.5 | 4 | 25.7 | 30 |
| Serials | 18.8 | 5 | 8.0 | 1 | 17.0 | 6 |
| Documents/Maps | 28.4 | 7 | 13.0 | 1 | 26.5 | 8 |
| Circulation | 17.2 | 17 | 12.2 | 6 | 15.9 | 23 |
| Rare Books/Manuscripts | 17.0 | 3 | . | | 17.0 | 3 |
| Computer Systems | 22.5 | 2 | 19.8 | 6 | 20.5 | 8 |
| Other | 18.0 | 23 | 15.8 | 9 | 17.4 | 32 |
| | | | | | | |
| Public services | 12.1 | 11 | 13.1 | 7 | 12.5 | 18 |
| Technical services | 11.5 | 13 | 14.3 | 4 | 12.2 | 17 |
| Administration | 15.6 | 8 | 25.0 | 1 | 16.7 | 9 |
| Reference | 12.1 | 138 | 10.6 | 78 | 11.6 | 216 |
| Cataloger | 19.8 | 33 | 17.7 | 9 | 19.3 | 42 |
| **All Positions** | **18.1** | **488** | **15.7** | **246** | **17.3** | **734** |

. No positions were reported in this category.

## Table 48: Number and Average Salaries of ARL University Law Librarians by Years of Experience and Sex, FY 2010–2011

| Experience | WOMEN | | MEN | | TOTAL | | % OF TOTAL |
|---|---|---|---|---|---|---|---|
| | Salary | No. | Salary | No. | Salary | No. | |
| 0–3 years | $57,382 | 62 | $59,278 | 34 | $58,054 | 96 | 13% |
| 4–7 years | 62,747 | 70 | 64,114 | 41 | 63,252 | 111 | 15% |
| 8–11 years | 69,850 | 39 | 69,083 | 28 | 69,530 | 67 | 9% |
| 12–15 years | 70,354 | 58 | 85,318 | 28 | 75,226 | 86 | 12% |
| 16–19 years | 71,967 | 49 | 87,101 | 23 | 76,801 | 72 | 10% |
| 20–23 years | 89,316 | 38 | 91,057 | 25 | 90,007 | 63 | 9% |
| 24–27 years | 85,832 | 35 | 89,627 | 23 | 87,337 | 58 | 8% |
| 28–31 years | 87,335 | 49 | 117,575 | 21 | 96,407 | 70 | 10% |
| 32–35 years | 95,806 | 43 | 113,406 | 21 | 101,581 | 64 | 9% |
| over 35 years | ‡ | 45 | ‡ | 2 | 100,273 | 47 | 6% |
| **All Positions** | **$77,036** | **488** | **$82,751** | **246** | **$78,951** | **734** | **100%** |

Canadian salaries are expressed in US dollars.
‡ Salary data are not published when fewer than four individuals are involved in either category.

# University Library Questionnaire and Instructions

## ASSOCIATION OF RESEARCH LIBRARIES

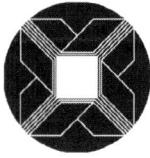

## ARL ANNUAL SALARY SURVEY 2010-11
### *University Library Questionnaire*
### GENERAL AND DATA INPUT (EXCEL) INSTRUCTIONS

## http://www.arl.org/stats/annualsurveys/salary/

### GENERAL OVERVIEW

- **Use the newly available Web form for your data submission:**
- University Libraries: http://www.formstack.com/forms/?987723-c6BynijupA
  Fill in Part I on the Web and upload your file for Part II through the same interface.
  NOTE: You must complete the entire submission in a single session. The Web interface does
  **NOT** allow you to return and edit your information once it is submitted.

- **This survey is concerned with professional positions only.** Since the criteria for determining
  professional status vary among libraries, there is no attempt to define the term "professional."
  Each library should report the salaries of those staff members it considers professionals,
  irrespective of faculty status or membership in a collective bargaining unit, including, when
  appropriate, staff who are not librarians in the strict sense of the term, such as computer
  experts, systems analysts, budget officers, etc.

- **Report individual salaries for the Main, Law, and Medical library on the separate template
  using Microsoft Excel (see http://www.arl.org/stats/annualsurveys/salary/salform10.shtml).**
  A generic template is available. Add your institution's ARL Library Institution Code [LibID].
  (See http://www.arl.org/stats/annualsurveys/surveycoord/instno_inam.shtml if you do
  not know your code.)

- **Use "Percent" to determine if an employee works full-time or part-time.** All full-time
  employees have Percent = 1.00, i.e., they work 100% of a full-time schedule. If Percent is less
  than 1.00, then the employee works that fraction of a full-time schedule. For example, a 65%
  time appointment would be entered as 0.65. Calculate the percent appointment by dividing
  the amount of time an employee works by the amount considered to be the norm for full-
  time employment at your institution. For example, if a full-time appointment at your
  institution is 12 months at 40 hours per week:
    - A 9-month part-time appointment has Percent = 9/12, or 0.75.
    - An appointment at 30 hours per week has Percent = 30/40, also 0.75.
    - An appointment at 30 hours and 9 months has Percent = 0.75 x 0.75 = 0.56.
  Enter Percent with two decimal points.

21 Dupont Circle NW, Suite 800
Washington, DC 20036
202 296 2296 telephone
202 872 0884 fax
http://www.arl.org

- **Report salaries for both full-time and part-time professional positions**. Salaries for part-time positions should **NOT** be converted to their full-time equivalents. Report the actual part-time salary paid and indicate the percent appointment for that employee in the appropriate column.

- **Include salaries for all professional positions, regardless of whether the salaries come from regular library budget funds <u>or from special funds such as research grants</u>**. Please include all professionals involved in the provision of library services, including **contract-supported positions**.

- **The salary figures should be straight gross salary figures. <u>Do not include fringe benefits</u>.**

- **Provide explanatory footnotes to the reported figures, when necessary, at the end of Part I.** Footnotes will be included in the published survey, where appropriate.

- **After all data have been entered, make a backup copy of the complete file for your institution's master file**. Your backup should include individual names/ID numbers. NOTE: The data submitted to ARL should NOT include individual names/ID numbers, so <u>ARL will NOT be able to supply a copy of your institution's complete file next year</u>.

- **Please return the questionnaire the ARL Statistics and Assessment Program by <u>October 1, 2010.</u> Be sure to keep a complete copy of your return, including the electronic version of the data for your files**.

## INSTRUCTIONS

### Part I: Summary Data (Microsoft Word Form)

1. Part I of this survey deals with general information for the current fiscal year, 2010-11.

2. Include the Beginning Professional Salary for Law and Medical libraries if included in the survey.

3. The Beginning Professional Salary is the salary that **would** be paid to a **newly hired professional without experience**, not necessarily the lowest professional salary paid. In reporting the beginning salary, please use a figure that is actually used or likely to be used for entry-level librarians hired by your library, even if it is your practice rarely to hire entry-level professionals without experience.

4. Please report the **2010-11** Beginning Professional Salary <u>to the best of your knowledge</u> as it exists on July 1, 2010. Do not delay returning your survey with the expectation that more information will be available later.

5. The 2010-11 Average and Median Salary figures will be calculated by ARL from the individual data supplied.

6. Be sure to fill in the name of the reporting library and the name of the person who prepares the report.

## Part II: Individual Data (Microsoft Excel Form)

1. Part II of this survey requests information on salary, sex, minority status, rank, and years of experience for all filled positions for fiscal year 2010-11. The survey requests information for individuals; aggregate data for each institution will be generated by computer. Vacant positions should be excluded from your report.

2. Data for the Main, Law, and Medical libraries should be reported on separate Excel files.

3. **Obtain the Excel file.** These instructions assume that you have Microsoft Excel available for use. If not, or if you have trouble opening the files in Excel, please call the ARL Statistics and Assessment Program at (202) 296-2296 or email stats@arl.org.

4. The template Excel file is available at: http://www.arl.org/stats/annualsurveys/salary/salform10.shtml. This is a generic, blank file that can hold data for Main, Law, or Medical libraries. The file's name is "sal10xxxx.xls"; open the file and save it to your own computer by choosing "Save As" under the File menu. When saving the file, utilize ARL as the prefix for main library reports, use 10 to designate the year (2010-11), and change the "xxxx" in its name to your ARL institution code number, e.g., "ARL101150.xls." Note: use MED for medical libraries, e.g. "MED101150" and LAW to denote law libraries, e.g., "LAW101150."

> The file contains columns labeled as follows:
> Required:  Name/ID# LibID Page Line Salary Job Sex OEOcat Yrsexp Rank Percent
> Optional:  YrBirth JobAdd LibDeg OthDeg YrsLib
> Optional:  Hisp NatAm Asian Black HawPI White

In the LibID column, enter your ARL Library Institution Code. (See http://www.arl.org/stats/annualsurveys/surveycoord/instno_inam.shtml if you do not know your code.) If you leave this column blank we will fill it in for you when we receive the data.

Columns labeled "Page," "Line," and "Percent" are already filled for you. The numbers in the "Page" and "Line" columns will be used to identify these positions in case of data errors; do not change them. Eleven "pages" of 25 lines each have been provided; if this is not sufficient to list all positions at your institution, copy and paste lines 1-25 of the last page as needed.

## Entering Data for Part II: Individual Data (Microsoft Excel Form)

1. The "Name/ID#" column is for your internal use, to enter and verify information for staff members by name. ARL does not require that you submit the information in this field to ARL. Please delete this column before sending the file to ARL. Upon receiving this file, ARL will delete any data in this column if you have not deleted them already.

2. The "LibID" will hold your institution's ARL number, for identification purposes. If you do not know your ARL number, you can find it on the Web under ARL Library Institution Codes. If you leave this column blank, it will be filled in by ARL staff.

3. "Salary" should be entered as it existed on July 1, 2010. Please do not hold up the reporting process for later salary adjustments. Include all filled positions and exclude all vacant positions. Report the actual salary paid. Do not adjust part-time salaries to their full-time equivalents; ARL will do this during the data analysis and verification stage. Do not include fringe benefits.

4. Each position can have only one "Job" code, to be taken from the following list:

| | |
|---|---|
| DIRLIB | Director of Libraries (includes Dean of Libraries and equivalent titles) |
| ASCDIR | Associate Director |
| ASTDIR | Assistant Director |
| HDMED | Head, Medical Library (Human Medicine only) |
| HDLAW | Head, Law Library |
| HDBR | Head, Other Branch Library (including Veterinary Medicine) |
| FSPEC | Functional Specialist |

| | | |
|---|---|---|
| | ARCH | Archivists/Curators |
| | BUSI | Budget/Fiscal/Business Manager/Facilities |
| | HUMRES | Human Resources/Training/Staff Development |
| | ITS | Information Technology Systems |
| | ITW | Information Technology Web Development |
| | ITP | Information Technology Programming/Application Development |
| | MEDIA | Media/Multimedia Specialists (including graphics) |
| | PRES | Preservation/Conservation |

| | |
|---|---|
| SSPEC | Subject Specialist |
| HDACQ | Head, Acquisitions Department |
| HDCAT | Head, Catalog Department/Unit |
| HDCIRC | Head, Circulation |
| HDCOMP | Head, Library and Computer Systems |
| HDDOC | Head, Documents Department |
| HDMAP | Head, Map Room/Department |
| HDRBM | Head, Rare Book/Manuscripts Department |
| HDREF | Head, Reference Department |
| HDSER | Head, Serials Department |
| HDOTH | Head, Other Department/Service/Agency |
| CAT | Catalogers, both general and specialized |
| REF | Reference librarians, both general and specialized |
| PUBS | Public Services, non-supervisory, except reference librarians |
| TECH | Technical Services, non-supervisory, except catalogers |
| ADMIN | Administrative and other units, non-supervisory position |

The position categories used in this survey are intended to correspond roughly with the activities carried on in libraries, not with any particular pattern of staff organization or nomenclature. Please use these categories in the manner you feel best applies to your library. If any individual has responsibilities described by more than one of the above categories, choose the category that is most typical of his/her general duties.

**Associate or Assistant Director, and Head, Other Branch**. Use these codes for all persons at these levels regardless of the area of specialty. If an assistant or associate director is also head of a department, choose the category that most reflects the general duties of the person currently in the position.

**Specialists.** These are of two kinds: Subject Specialists primarily build collections, but may also offer specialized reference and bibliographic services; Functional Specialists are media specialists or experts in management fields such as personnel, fiscal matters, systems, preservation, etc. Specialists may not be, strictly speaking, professional librarians (i.e., have an MLS). The "specialist" category would generally not be used for someone with significant supervisory responsibilities, who should instead be listed as a department head or assistant director (see also note under Assistant Department Head, below).

**Functional Specialist sub-codes.** Starting with the 2004-05 Salary Survey, the ARL Statistics and Assessment Committee adopted a proposal from the ACRL Personnel Administrators and Staff Development Officers Discussion Group to break down the Functional Specialist category. For each position which would have been labeled FSPEC prior to 2004-05, instead please use one of the eight sub-codes (ARCH, BUSI, HUMRES, ITS, ITW, ITP, MEDIA, PRES) to describe that position. If you cannot determine which sub-code to use, please use the FSPEC code.

**Department Heads.** Department Heads not specifically included in the above list should be included under the category "Head, Other Department/Service/Agency." Head, Catalog Department should be used either for the department that handles all cataloging, or for the head of a specialized cataloging unit (e.g. copy cataloging or foreign languages). List the head of library automation and computer systems, applications, programming, etc. as HDCOMP unless that person is also an Associate or Assistant Director, in which case use the appropriate administrative code. If there is an intermediate level of management between an Associate or Assistant Director and the professionals who actually carry out the analysis, programming, etc., use HDCOMP to define that intermediate level. Professionals who carry out analysis, programming, etc., should be listed as functional specialists (FSPEC).

**Head, Acquisitions Department.** Use HDACQ for all of the following positions: (a) head of a department that is responsible for the selection of material (or management of selection activities carried out on a basis encompassing more than a single organizational unit), but not responsible for the placement of orders, payment of invoices, etc.; (b) head of a department responsible for the placement of orders, maintaining on-order files, payment of invoices, etc., but not responsible for selection decisions; (c) head of a department responsible for both the selection decisions (or coordination of selection activities) and for acquiring the material. Libraries that split these two functions between two departments should report more than one professional with the position HDACQ.

*Special note concerning Assistant Department Heads.* Assistant Department Heads who are responsible for major units and spend the bulk of their time in supervision and revision of the work of others should also be listed as "Head, Other Department/Service/Agency." See additional subcodes below for Head, Cataloging, and Head, Other Department. However, Assistant Head positions responsible for small units or for supervision only in the absence of the head should be reported as non-supervisory or specialist positions as appropriate.]

**Administrative.** Please note that ADMIN is not only for Administrative Services and related positions, but also can be applied to Public Relations/Communications,

Development/Fundraising, and all other administrative and/or professional positions which do not have a logical home elsewhere.

5.**Please indicate "Sex" with the letter M or F**, indicating male or female, respectively.

6. **"OEOCat" minority status code**, for U.S. university libraries only, should be indicated with one of the following code numbers.  (Leave blank if a Canadian library):

        1 = Black
        2 = Hispanic
        3 = Asian or Pacific Islander
        4 = American Indian or Native Alaskan
        5 = Caucasian/Other

7. **"YrsExp," or total years of professional experience.**  For most professional staff members this will mean counting the years since the MLS degree was awarded.  When counting, do not subtract interim periods when an individual was not engaged in professional library employment if these periods are short in relation to the overall professional career.  Count an academic year contract period as a full year.  Be sure to include professional experience in previous positions and in other institutions.  The figure should be rounded off to the nearest whole number; for example, a position with 14.5 years of experience would appear as 15.

8. **Indicate "Rank" using the following system of codes**:
0      The library director.  Some systems also use 0 for assistant and/or associate directors.
1      Lowest level in the rank structure, such as an entry-level position.
2-8   Successively higher levels; for example, 5 indicates a higher rank than 2.
9      Rank cannot be determined, or, the individual is outside the organization's rank structure.

Responses concerning rank should be limited to professional librarians, and other professionals who occupy the same ranks as librarians.  Leave the rank column blank for professionals who do not occupy these ranks or if the column is not applicable.  For example, if the Library Business Officer holds a rank typically used for university administrators but not for librarians, do not supply a rank code for that individual, even if you have included salary and other data.

If multiple ranking structures are used for librarians and these structures are substantially different and not equivalent, enter individual rank information only for that group which represents the largest fraction of "rank-and-file" librarians.

The maximum number of ranks reported here should not exceed the maximum number of rank-levels reported in Part I for individual data under Rank structure.  When counting the total number of rank levels, include ranks that may be unoccupied at the present time due to circumstances like unusually high turnover, hiring freezes, etc.

9. **"Percent"** is used to determine if an employee works full-time or part-time.  All full-time employees have Percent = 1.00, i.e., they work 100% of a full-time schedule.  If Percent is less than 1.00, then the employee works that fraction of a full-time schedule.  For example, a 65% time appointment would be entered as 0.65. Calculate the percent appointment by dividing the amount of time an employee works by the amount considered to be the norm for full-time

employment at your institution.  For example, if a full-time appointment at your institution is 12 months at 40 hours per week:

- o A 9-month part-time appointment has Percent = 9/12, or 0.75.
- o An appointment at 30 hours per week has Percent = 30/40, also 0.75.
- o An appointment at 30 hours and 9 months has Percent = 0.75 x 0.75 = 0.56.

Enter Percent with two decimal points.

*Optional Questions:*  (Shown on printed forms as the last 11 columns)

1. **Year of Birth (YrBirth).**  For each individual, record the four-digit year of birth.

2. **Position Code Addenda (JobAdd).**  Use this column to provide additional information only for the following position categories:

a. **Associate and Assistant Directors** (ASCDIR and ASTDIR).  For each category, indicate if the person has a defined area of responsibility using the codes below.  Use the code that most closely reflects the general duties of the person in the position.

| | |
|---|---|
| Administrative Services | ADM |
| Collection Development | CDV |
| Other (or unspecified) | OTH |
| Public Services | PBS |
| Systems/Automation | SYS |
| Technical Services | TS |

b. **Head, Other Branch Library** (HDBR).  Use the codes below to indicate the subject area of the branch:

| | |
|---|---|
| Humanities/Fine Arts | HFA |
| Other | OTH |
| Science & Tech. | SCI |
| Social/Behavioral Sci. | SBS |
| Undergraduate Library | UGL |

c. **Functional Specialists** (FSPEC).  Indicate any non-supervisory staff who are primarily responsible for the following activities using the codes below:

| | |
|---|---|
| Acquisitions | ACQ |
| Development Officer | DVP |
| Interlibrary Loan | ILL |
| Marketing/Communications | COM |
| Serials | SER |

d. **Subject Specialists, Reference Librarians, Catalogers, and Public Services** (SSPEC, REF, CAT, PUBS).  Use these codes to indicate non-supervisory main and/or branch library staff who specialize in <u>one</u> of the following subject areas (either a sub-field, or the entire area).  Do not add codes for staff in these positions who have broader, other, or mixed subject responsibilities (e.g. more than one field specialty); but do include subject specialists who also have some (i.e. 50% or less) general or other assignments.

| | |
|---|---|
| Humanities/Fine Arts | HFA |
| Science & Tech. | SCI |

Social/Behavioral Sci.    SBS
Undergraduate Library    UGL

e. **Head, Cataloging Department/Unit** (HDCAT). Use the codes below to indicate whether the person is the head of the entire cataloging department for the library, or the head of a specialized unit. If the person is head of the whole department, repeat the same HDCAT code as in the earlier column.

| | |
|---|---|
| Head, all cataloging | HDCAT |
| Head, copy cataloging | HDC |
| Head, foreign languages | HDF |
| Head, non-book formats | HDN |
| Head, serials cat. | HDS |
| Head, other special cat. | HDO |

f. **Head, Other Department/Service/Agency** (HDOTH). For heads of departments not given a separate category in the major list, please add one of the following codes:

| | |
|---|---|
| Audio Visual/Media | AVM |
| Archivist | ARC |
| Business/Personnel Office | BPO |
| Other | OTH |
| Interlibrary Loan | ILL |
| Preservation | PRS |

3. **Library degrees earned (LibDeg).** Use the following codes to indicate the highest academic degree earned in the field of librarianship:

| | |
|---|---|
| 0 | None |
| 1 | Bachelor |
| 2 | Master |
| 3 | CAGS (6th yr. certificate) |
| 4 | Doctorate (Other than Ph.D.) |
| 5 | Ph.D. |

4. **Other degrees earned (OtherDeg).** Use the following codes to indicate the highest degree earned in fields other than librarianship, including basic undergraduate education:

| | |
|---|---|
| 0 | None |
| 1 | Bachelor |
| 2 | Master |
| 3 | Second Master (i.e., 2 subject fields) |
| 4 | CAGS (6th-year certificate) |
| 5 | LLB/JD |
| 6 | Doctorate (Other than Ph.D.) |
| 7 | Ph.D. |

5. **Years of professional experience at reporting institution (YrsLib).** Use this line to report the number of years of professional experience each librarian has had at your institution. This figure should not exceed the number reported as Total Years of Professional Experience on the main part of the form.

6. Please complete as much of this section as possible (US libraries only), but do not hold up the reporting process if some of the data requested are not available. Canadian libraries should leave these columns blank. The major change in the revised standard for the classification of federal data on race and ethnicity is that now respondents are able to report more than one race by choosing multiple responses to the following questions

*Race and Ethnicity:* The U.S. Office of Management and Budget has revised the Standards for the Classification of Federal Data on Race and Ethnicity and according to the new standard there will be five minimum categories for data on race (American Indian or Alaska Native, Asian, Black or African American, Native Hawaiian or Other Pacific Islander, and White) and one category for data on ethnicity ("Hispanic or Latino"). **Respondents will be able to report more than one race by choosing multiple responses to the race question.** The purpose of the revised classification is to reflect the increasing diversity of the U.S. population that has resulted primarily from growth in immigration and in interracial marriages. The new standards were used by the Bureau of the Census in the 2000 decennial census.[1] In light of these developments, we are collecting the new classification on race and ethnicity in the *ARL Annual Salary Survey on an **optional** basis.*

**Ethnicity** should be indicated by coding 1 to indicate if the person is of Hispanic or Latino ethnicity, and coding 0 otherwise. The definition of Hispanic or Latino ethnicity is: A person of Cuban, Mexican, Puerto Rican, Cuban, South or Central American, or other Spanish culture or origin, regardless of race.

**Race** should be indicated for U.S. university libraries only, by choosing one or more responses among the five racial categories provided here; 1=yes and 0=no. You can select multiple racial categories for a person. The definitions of the five racial categories, listed with their respective column names, are:

American Indian or Alaska Native (NatAm): A person having origins in any of the original peoples of North and South America (including Central America) who maintains tribal affiliation or community attachment.

Asian (Asian): A person having origins in any of the original peoples of the Far East, Southeast Asia, or the Indian subcontinent including, for example, Cambodia, China, India, Japan, Korea, Malaysia, Pakistan, the Philippine Islands, Thailand, and Vietnam.

Black or African American (Black): A person having origins in any of the black racial groups of Africa.

Native Hawaiian or Other Pacific Islander (HawPI): A person having origins in any of the original peoples of Hawaii, Guam, Samoa, or other Pacific Islands.

White (White): A person having origins in any of the original peoples of Europe, the Middle East, or North Africa.

---

[1] http://www.census.gov/population/www/socdemo/race/racefactcb.html

## Submitting the Data for Part I and Part II on the Web

ARL is using the online services of FormStack to collect the data. As part of its privacy policy, FormStack pledges not to sell any collected information to third parties. For the complete FormStack privacy policy, visit http://www.formstack.com/privacy.html. ARL also accepts Part I and Part II of the salary survey by e-mail from those users who may be uncomfortable submitting the files in FormStack:

- University Libraries: http://www.formstack.com/forms/?987723-c6BynijupA

Be sure to have the electronic copy of your completed salary survey Excel file handy as you will be submitting this file via the FormStack Web form. In addition to the completed Excel file, be prepared to provide the following information as well:

- The name, title, email and phone number of the person who prepared the Excel file. The name, title, email and phone number of your institution's contact person for the salary survey (if different from the person who prepared the Excel file)

- Indicate whether you are submitting salary information for one or more of the following: Main, Law, or Medical library, and the beginning professional salary and rank structure for each.

- **For professional salary** list the salary that would be paid to a newly hired professional without experience (even if local practice discourages hiring entry-level professionals without experience). Please report the 2010-11 beginning professional salary to the best of your knowledge as it existed on July 1, 2010.

- **For rank structure**, list the number of unique levels in your institution's rank structure. If you have no levels in your rank structure, use 1. The number reported here should be equal to the highest number in the "Rank" column of your Excel file (i.e., the number of levels reported in your Excel file should equal the number of levels reported here).

- The names of the libraries that are included and excluded in your figures for the 'general libraries' (these can be main campus libraries or branch campus libraries), as well as any other explanatory information, should be indicated in a footnote. In your footnotes, report any information that would clarify the figures submitted: the inclusion and exclusion of branch campus libraries, a reporting date that is sooner/later than July 1, 2010, etc. Please make an effort to word your footnotes in a manner consistent with notes appearing in the published report, so that ARL can interpret your footnotes correctly.

Please return the completed questionnaire to the
ARL Statistics and Assessment Program by **October 1, 2010.**

For assistance, contact Martha Kyrillidou (martha@arl.org), Shaneka Morris (shaneka@arl.org), Gary Roebuck (gary@arl.org) or David Green (david@arl.org).
Tel: 202-296-2296 or Fax: 202-872-0884.
## http://www.arl.org/stats/annualsurveys/salary/

# ARL ANNUAL SALARY SURVEY 2010-11
## UNIVERSITY LIBRARY QUESTIONNAIRE

Note: This is a copy of the form that you will submit electronically at:
http://www.formstack.com/forms/?987723-c6BynijupA

**Part I: Summary Data**

Reporting Institution _____ Date Returned to ARL _____

Report Prepared by (name) _____

Title _____

Email address _____ Phone number _____

Contact person (if different) _____

Title _____

Email address _____ Phone number _____

*(Note: ARL will calculate the **2010-11 median and average** professional salaries for your library from the individual data you supply in Part II (Excel form) of this questionnaire.)*

| 1. | **Beginning Professional Salary** | **Main** | **Law** | **Health** |
|---|---|---|---|---|
| | Beginning professional salary for 2010-11 | _____ | _____ | _____ |

**(Note:** *The Information shown below must be completed for all three branches (i.e. Main, Law and Health Science Libraries) in Part1 of the online form).*

2.    **Rank Structure**.

Indicate the number of levels in your institution's rank structure for professional librarians. You should report here the maximum number of rank levels, reported in Part II for individual data, under the Rank column.

_____ 1 level (i.e., no differentiated levels)

_____ 2 levels

_____ 3 levels

_____ 4 levels

_____ 5 levels

_____ more than 5 levels (please specify the number of levels: _____)

## 3.   FOOTNOTES

**3a.** Please list which libraries are included in the data submitted for the "general" libraries.  These can be main campus libraries or branch campus libraries.

**3b.** Please list which libraries are NOT included in the data submitted for the "general" libraries.  These can be main campus libraries or branch campus libraries.

Please indicate any other explanatory information in footnotes. These additional footnotes, if necessary, should be placed in the space below or on attached pages.

Please submit the completed questionnaire to the web form at:
http://www.formstack.com/forms/?987723-c6BynijupA
by **October 1, 2010.**

For assistance, contact Martha Kyrillidou (martha@arl.org), Shaneka Morris (shaneka@arl.org), Gary Roebuck
(gary@arl.org) or David Green (david@arl.org).
Tel: 202-296-2296 or Fax: 202-872-0884

## ARL ANNUAL SALARY SURVEY 2010-11
*UNIVERSITY LIBRARY QUESTIONNAIRE*

### Part II: Individual Data

*Note: This is a copy of the Excel form that you will submit electronically at:*
http://www.formstack.com/forms/?987723-c6BynijupA

| Confidential *Detach or delete before mailing to the ARL Office* Name/ID# | Year | LibID | Page | Line | Salary | Job | Sex | OEOCat | YrsExp | Rank | Percent | YrBirth | Job Add | Lib Deg | Oth Deg | Yrs Lib | Hisp | Nat Am | Asian | Black | Haw PI | White |
|---|---|---|---|---|---|---|---|---|---|---|---|---|---|---|---|---|---|---|---|---|---|---|
| | 2010 | | 1 | 1 | | | | | | | 1 | | | | | | | | | | | |
| | 2010 | | 1 | 2 | | | | | | | 1 | | | | | | | | | | | |
| | 2010 | | 1 | 3 | | | | | | | 1 | | | | | | | | | | | |
| | 2010 | | 1 | 4 | | | | | | | 1 | | | | | | | | | | | |
| | 2010 | | 1 | 5 | | | | | | | 1 | | | | | | | | | | | |
| | 2010 | | 1 | 6 | | | | | | | 1 | | | | | | | | | | | |
| | 2010 | | 1 | 7 | | | | | | | 1 | | | | | | | | | | | |
| | 2010 | | 1 | 8 | | | | | | | 1 | | | | | | | | | | | |
| | 2010 | | 1 | 9 | | | | | | | 1 | | | | | | | | | | | |
| | 2010 | | 1 | 10 | | | | | | | 1 | | | | | | | | | | | |
| | 2010 | | 1 | 11 | | | | | | | 1 | | | | | | | | | | | |
| | 2010 | | 1 | 12 | | | | | | | 1 | | | | | | | | | | | |
| | 2010 | | 1 | 13 | | | | | | | 1 | | | | | | | | | | | |
| | 2010 | | 1 | 14 | | | | | | | 1 | | | | | | | | | | | |
| | 2010 | | 1 | 15 | | | | | | | 1 | | | | | | | | | | | |
| | 2010 | | 1 | 16 | | | | | | | 1 | | | | | | | | | | | |
| | 2010 | | 1 | 17 | | | | | | | 1 | | | | | | | | | | | |
| | 2010 | | 1 | 18 | | | | | | | 1 | | | | | | | | | | | |
| | 2010 | | 1 | 19 | | | | | | | 1 | | | | | | | | | | | |
| | 2010 | | 1 | 20 | | | | | | | 1 | | | | | | | | | | | |

Duplicate this sheet if you need additional lines. Please return to the ARL Statistics and Measurement Program by **October 1, 2010.**

For assistance, contact Martha Kyrillidou (martha@arl.org), Shaneka Morris (shaneka@arl.org), Gary Roebuck (gary@arl.org) or David Green (david@arl.org).
Tel: 202-296-2296 or Fax: 202-872-0884

# NONUNIVERSITY LIBRARY QUESTIONNAIRE AND INSTRUCTIONS

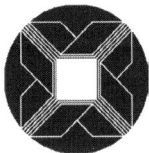

# ASSOCIATION OF RESEARCH LIBRARIES

## ARL ANNUAL SALARY SURVEY 2010-11
### NONUNIVERSITY LIBRARY QUESTIONNAIRE

### General Instructions for Completing the Questionnaire

1. This survey is concerned with the salaries of professional positions only. Since the criteria for determining professional status vary among libraries, there is no attempt to define the term "professional." Each library should report the salaries of those staff members it considers professionals, irrespective of membership in a collective bargaining unit, and including, when appropriate, staff who are not librarians in the strict sense of the term, such as systems analysts, budget officers, etc.

2. **Obtain the Word file.** These instructions assume that you have Microsoft Word available for use. If not, or if you have trouble opening the files in Word, please call the ARL Statistics and Assessment Program at (202) 296-2296 or email stats@arl.org.

3. The template Word file is available at: http://www.arl.org/stats/annualsurveys/salary/salform10.shtml. This is a generic, blank form that can hold your data. The file's name is "sal10_nuform.doc"; open the file and save it to your own computer by choosing "Save As" under the File menu. When saving the file, utilize ARL as the prefix, use 10 to designate the year (2010-11), and change the "xxxx" in its name to your ARL institution code number, e.g., "ARL109975.doc."

4. Salaries should be reported for all filled positions. Vacant positions should be excluded from your report.

5. Report 2010-11 salaries *as they exist on July 1, 2010*. If the library normally increases salaries at a date after July l, and the salary as of that later date is known or can be estimated (within $100 or so) by the time the questionnaire is due to be returned, please use the higher salary and footnote the effective date and/or whether the reported figures are known or estimated. Please do not hold up the reporting process for later salary adjustments.

6. The Median Salary is the salary that has an equal number of salaries above it and below it. In those libraries with an even number of positions, the median salary is the average of the two salaries that have an equal number of salaries above and below them.

7. The Beginning Professional Salary is the salary that would be paid to a professional without experience, not necessarily the lowest professional salary paid. In reporting the beginning salary, please use a figure that is actually used or likely to be used for entry-level librarians hired by your library.

8. Salaries should be reported for both full-time and part-time professional positions. However, salaries for part-time positions should be converted to their full-time equivalents before reporting; do not report the actual part-time salary paid.

9. Salaries should normally be reported on a 12-month basis. If an appointment is for 9 or 10 months at the option of the employee, the actual salary paid should be increased to its 12-month equivalent. However, if appointments of less than 12 months are required by the employer, report the actual salary paid.

10. The salaries for all professional positions should be included, regardless of whether the salaries come from regular library budget funds or from special funds such as research grants.

11. The salary figures should be straight gross salary figures. Do not include fringe benefits.

12. Explanatory footnotes to the reported figures may be provided when necessary. Footnotes will be included in the published survey.

13. Provide the name of the reporting library and the name of the person who prepares the report.

14. On the second page of the questionnaire (Part II) indicate the number of filled professional positions in each salary range for fiscal years 2009-10 and 2010-11.

15. **Use the newly available Web form for your data submission:**
(http://www.formstack.com/forms/?987727-c6BynijupA). Fill in Part I on the Web and upload your file for Part II through the same interface. NOTE: You must complete the entire submission in a single session. The Web interface does **NOT** allow you to return and edit your information once it is submitted.

Note: ARL is using the online services of FormStack to collect the data. As part of its privacy policy, FormStack pledges not to sell any collected information to third parties. For the complete FormStack privacy policy, visit http://www.formstack.com/privacy.html. ARL also accepts Part I and Part II of the salary survey by e-mail attachment from those users who may be uncomfortable submitting the files in FormStack.

**Please Submit the Web form by October 1, 2010.**

For assistance, contact Martha Kyrillidou (martha@arl.org), Shaneka Morris (shaneka@arl.org), Gary Roebuck (gary@arl.org) or David Green (david@arl.org).
Tel: 202-296-2296 or Fax: 202-872-0884

# ARL ANNUAL SALARY SURVEY 2010-11
## NONUNIVERSITY LIBRARY QUESTIONNAIRE

Note: This is a copy of the form that you will submit electronically at:
http://www.formstack.com/forms/?987727-c6BynijupA

**Part I: Summary Data**

Reporting Institution _____ Date Returned to ARL _____

Report Prepared by (name) _____

Title _____

Email address _____ Phone number_____

Contact person (if different) _____

Title _____

Email address_____ Phone number_____

1.  Complete the table on the back of this sheet by indicating the number of filled or temporarily vacant professional positions in each salary range for fiscal years 2009-10 and 2010-11.

2.  Median professional salary for fiscal year 2010-11:  _____

3.  Beginning professional salary for 2010-11:  _____

4.  Footnotes (please compare with footnotes from surveys of previous years)

    a.  Law Library salaries are included.

        _____ Yes          _____ No          _____ We do not have a Law Library.

    b.  Medical Library salaries are included.

        _____ Yes          _____ No          _____ We do not have a Medical Library.

    c.  Branch libraries not included (please attach an additional sheet if necessary):

        _____

        _____

5.  Other comments (please attach an additional sheet if necessary):

        _____

        _____

## Part II Salaries:

Indicate the number of filled professional positions in each salary range for fiscal years 2009-10 and 2010-11.

| | Number of Positions | |
|---|---|---|
| Salary Range | 2009-10 | 2010-11 |
| More than 300,000 | | |
| 250,000 - 299,999 | | |
| 200,000 - 250,000 | | |
| 175,000 - 199,999 | | |
| 150,000 - 174,999 | | |
| 140,000 - 149,999 | | |
| 130,000 - 139,999 | | |
| 120,000 - 129,999 | | |
| 110,000 - 119,999 | | |
| 100,000 - 109,999 | | |
| 95,000 - 99,999 | | |
| 90,000 - 94,999 | | |
| 85,000 - 89,999 | | |
| 80,000 - 84,999 | | |
| 79,000 - 79,999 | | |
| 78,000 - 78,999 | | |
| 76,000 - 77,999 | | |
| 74,000 - 75,999 | | |
| 72,000 - 73,999 | | |
| 70,000 - 71,999 | | |
| 68,000 - 69,999 | | |
| 66,000 - 67,999 | | |
| 64,000 - 65,999 | | |
| 62,000 - 63,999 | | |
| 60,000 - 61,999 | | |
| 58,000 - 59,999 | | |
| 56,000 - 57,999 | | |
| 54,000 - 55,999 | | |
| 52,000 - 53,999 | | |
| 50,000 - 51,999 | | |
| 48,000 - 49,999 | | |
| 46,000 - 47,999 | | |
| 44,000 - 45,999 | | |
| 42,000 - 43,999 | | |
| 40,000 - 41,999 | | |
| 38,000 - 39,999 | | |
| 36,000 - 37,999 | | |
| 34,000 - 35,999 | | |
| less than 34,000 | | |
| Total Number of Positions | | |

Please submit the completed questionnaire to the web form at:
http://www.formstack.com/forms/?987727-c6BynijupA
by **October 1, 2010.**

For assistance, contact Martha Kyrillidou (martha@arl.org), Shaneka Morris (shaneka@arl.org), Gary Roebuck (gary@arl.org) or David Green (david@arl.org).
Tel: 202-296-2296 or Fax: 202-872-0884

# Footnotes to the ARL Annual Salary Survey, 2010–2011

**All data is as of 1 July 2010 unless otherwise noted.**

## ALABAMA

Libraries included: Amelia Gayle Gorgas Library, Angelo Bruno Business Library, Eric and Sarah Rodgers Library for Science and Engineering, McLure Education Library, W.S. Hoole Special Collections Library.

## ALBERTA

Libraries included: Bibliographic and Information Technology Services, HT Coutts Education Library, Humanities & Social Sciences Library, Faculty Saint-Jean Library, Winspear Business Reference Library, Office of Staff Development & Training, Cameron Library (including Financial Systems & Analysis, Science & Technology Library, Information Technology Services and Research and Special Collections Services), Access Services (including Document Delivery and Interlibrary Loans).

## ARIZONA

Libraries included: Main Library, Science-Engineering Library, Fine Arts Library, Special Collections, Center for Creative Photography.

Data for the Medical library includes the Arizona Health Sciences Library (AHSL) in Tucson and AHSL on the Phoenix Biomedical Campus.

## ARIZONA STATE

Libraries included: Tempe Campus Library, Music Library, Architecture Library, Science Library, Downtown Campus, East Campus, West Campus.

## AUBURN

Libraries included: Main Library, Architecture Library & Vet Med Library.

## BOSTON

Libraries included: Mugar Memorial Library (Main), Library Theology, and the Gotlieb Archival Research Center.

There are eight levels in the Main and Law library's rank structures.

## BOSTON COLLEGE

Libraries included: O'Neill Library (main library), Educational Resource Center, Social Work Library, Theology and Ministry Library, Bapst Art Library, Burns Library.

## BRITISH COLUMBIA

Libraries included: Art+Architecture+Planning; Asian Library; David Lam Management Library; Education Library; Irving K. Barber Learning Centre (IKBLC); Koerner Library (Humanities & Social Sciences; Borrower Services); Music Library; Okanagan Library; Rare Books and Special Collections; Robson Square (UBC Library at Robson Square); Science and Engineering; University Archives; Xwi7xwa Library (First Nations House of Learning). Note: Technical Services and Systems are included in IKBLC and Woodward.

Libraries not included: Reading Rooms and Affiliated Libraries.

The University of British Columbia is still negotiating the 2010-2011 contract for faculty/librarians.

## BROWN

Libraries included: John D. Rockefeller Library, John Hay Library, Orwig Music Library, Sciences Library, List Art Center, John Carter Brown Library.

## CALGARY

Libraries included: MacKimmie Library, Gallagher Library of Geology & Geophysics; Business Library; Health Information Network Knowledge Centres; Military Museum Library & Archives; Doucette Library of Teaching Resources (Education Library).

## CALIFORNIA, BERKELEY

Libraries included: Doe, Moffitt, Bancroft, Anthropology, Art History/Classics, Astronomy-Mathematics-Statistics, Bioscience & Natural Resources, Business & Economics, Chemistry, C.V. Starr East Asian Library (including Center for Chinese Studies), Earth Sciences, Education-Psychology, Engineering, Environmental Design, Music, Optometry, Physics, Public Health (including Health Sciences Information Services & Occupational & Environmental Health), Social Welfare, & the Northern Regional Library Facility.

Libraries not included: Architecture Visual Resources/CED Visual Resource Center, Continuing Education of the Bar, Earthquake Engineering Research Center, Environmental Design Archives, Ethnic Studies, Giannini Foundation of Agricultural Economics, Institute of Government Studies, Institute for Research on Labor & Employment, Institute of Transportation Studies, Water Resources Center Archives. Also various departmental libraries: e.g. French, History, Philosophy, Rhetoric, Slavic Languages & Literature.

Beginning 2004-05, UCB salary figures include administrative stipends, where applicable.

There are six levels in the University of California, Berkeley's rank structure.

## CALIFORNIA, DAVIS

Libraries included: Peter J. Shields Library (Davis Campus); Physical Sciences & Engineering Library (Davis Campus); Agricultural & Resource Economics Library (Davis Campus).

Librarians who are department heads have received administrative stipends since July 1, 1999, but the stipends were not included in the salaries reported to ARL until the 2009-10 Salary Survey. We are including those stipends in the department head's salaries (as reported), and we plan to do so in the future.

## CALIFORNIA, LOS ANGELES

Libraries included: The Arts Library, College Library (Undergraduate Library), Eugene and Maxine Rosenfeld Management Library, Music Library, Richard C. Rudolph East Asian Library, Science & Engineering Library, Social Sciences and Humanities Library (Charles E. Young Research Library), and the Southern Regional Library Facility. Includes data for 12 affiliated libraries on the UCLA campus including the 1) American Indian Studies Center, 2) Ralph M. Bunche African American Studies Center, 3) Asian American Studies Center, 4) Chicano Studies Research Center, 5) Ethnomusicology Archive, 6) Film & Television Archive, 7) Graduate School of Education & Information Studies, Department of Information Studies, 8) Institute for Social Science Research, 9) Latin American Center/Hispanic American Periodicals Index, 10) Olive View Medical Center, 11) Grace M. Hunt English Reading Room, and 12) William Andrews Clark Memorial Library.

Librarians who are department heads have received administrative stipends since January 1998; however, these stipends were not included in the salaries reported to ARL prior to 2003. Beginning with the 2003 survey, UCLA now includes those stipends in salaries reported for department heads. Interim department heads also receive stipends and these are reported in the survey.

The General Library Survey includes one Council of Library & Information Resources (CLIR) Fellow.

Data for Louise M. Darling Biomedical Library includes information for the Pacific Southwest Regional Medical Library, an NLM-funded program that is part of the National Network/Libraries of Medicine based in the Biomedical Library.

## CALIFORNIA, RIVERSIDE

Libraries included: Rivera Library: (serving the College of Humanities, Arts and Social Sciences, School of Education, and the School of Business Administration). Orbach Science Library: (serving the College of Natural & Agricultural Sciences, the College of Engineering, and Biomedical Sciences).

Libraries not included: Media and Music Libraries are not included (there are no librarian employees in these facilities).

## CALIFORNIA, SAN DIEGO

Libraries included: Arts, Social Sciences & Humanities, Science & Engineering, International Relations & Pacific Studies, Scripps Institution of Oceanography, Center for Library & Instructional Services.

## CALIFORNIA, SANTA BARBARA

Libraries included: The Main and Arts Libraries.

There are eight levels in the University of California, Santa Barbara's rank structure.

## CANADA INSTITUTE OF SCIENTIFIC AND TECHNICAL INFORMATION

Figures for 2009 have not been included. The organization underwent a major restructuring and staff fluctuated considerably during this period.

## CASE WESTERN RESERVE

Libraries included: Kelvin Smith Library, Kulas Music Library, Mandel School of Applied Social Sciences Library and the Harris Library.

## CHICAGO

Libraries included: All libraries including law and medicine, are represented in "Main," we do not differentiate branches, and all librarians are included in the same salary scale and rank structure.

## CINCINNATI

Libraries included: All University of Cincinnati Libraries including the main library, eight college and departmental libraries (Archives and Rare Books; Chemistry-Biology; Classics; Design, Architecture, Art and Planning; Education, Criminal Justice and Human Services; Engineering and Applied Science; Geology-Mathematics-Physics; and Music),and two regional campus libraries (Clermont College and Raymond Walters College).

## COLORADO

Libraries included: Norlin Library (main), Music, Business, Math/Physics, Engineering, Earth Sciences.

The Beginning Professional Salary (BPS) reported for the Law Library is for librarians with an MLS alone. The beginning salary for librarians with an MLS and JD is $54,000.

## COLUMBIA

Libraries included: All libraries.

## CONNECTICUT

Libraries included: Homer Babbidge Library, Archives and Special Collections; Music and Dramatic Arts, Pharmacy, Avery Point Campus, Greater Hartford Campus, Stamford Campus, Torrington Campus, Waterbury Campus.

## CORNELL

Libraries included: Africana, Engineering/Physical Sciences, Entomology, Fine Arts, Geneva Experiment Station, Hotel Administration, Management, Mann Library, Math, Music, ILR, Olin/Kroch/Uris, Veterinary Medicine.

## DARTMOUTH

Libraries included: Baker-Berry Library, Sherman Art Library, Feldberg Business & Engineering Library, Paddock Music Library, Kresge Physical Sciences Library, Rauner Special Collections Library.

## DUKE

Libraries included: Perkins/Bostock, Lilly, Rare Book, Manuscript and Special Collections, Music, Divinity.

Duke University did not provide a merit pool for Fiscal Year 2011 (1 July 2010 - 30 June 2011). In general, any salary increases are the result in Fiscal Year 2011 of promotion, market adjustment, internal equity adjustment or compression adjustment.

## EMORY

Libraries included: Main, Theology, Business and Oxford College Library.

## FLORIDA

Libraries included: Humanities and Social Sciences, Science, Music, Journalism, Education, Architecture/Fine Arts, Special/Area Studies Collections.

There are six levels in the Main library's rank structure.

## FLORIDA STATE

Libraries included: Main Branch, Engineering and Science.

Libraries not included: Music, Career Center, Art (Ringling), School of Library and Information Studies, Panama City, FL Branch, Panama City, Panama Branch.

We have a six-level rank system: 0- Dean; 1- Assistant Instructor; 2- Associate Instructor; 3- Instruction librarian; 4- Assistant Librarian; 5- Associate Librarian; 6- University Librarian.

## GEORGE WASHINGTON

Libraries included: Gelman.

## GEORGETOWN

Libraries included: Bio-ethics.

There are nine levels in the health science library's rank structure.

## GEORGIA

Libraries included: Main Library, Science Library, Map Library, Student Learning Center Library, Curriculum Learning Center Library, several reading rooms and experimental station libraries located throughout the State of Georgia.

The University of Georgia Law Library has nine levels in its rank structure.

## GEORGIA TECH

Libraries included: Main library, Architecture library.

## GUELPH

Libraries included: Main Campus Libraries: McLaughlin Library; Branch Campus Libraries: Ridgetown Campus Library.
All salary values were reported in Canadian Dollars ($CAD).

Individual rank data have been included only for professional librarians. Rank structure as follows: Library Director assigned rank = 0; Assistant Librarian assigned rank = 1; Associate Librarian assigned rank = 2; Librarian assigned rank = 3; Non-librarian professionals assigned rank = 9.

Seven (7) Non-librarian professional positions are now co-funded by the Library budget (0.52 FTE).

## HARVARD

Libraries included: All libraries.

Salary rank structure includes ten levels.

## HAWAII

There are four levels in the Main library's rank structure: rank II to rank V. Rank I only applies to Instructional Faculty not Bibliographic Faculty.

There are four levels in the Law and Health Science library's rank structure: rank II–rank V.

## HOUSTON

The following are included: M.D. Anderson Library, Architecture and Art Library, Music Library, Weston A. Pettey Optometry Library.

The University of Houston Pharmacy Library was closed last year. The collection was incorporated into the MD Anderson Library collection.

## HOWARD

Libraries included: Founders Library, Undergraduate Library; the Architecture, Business, Divinity, and Social Work (branch) Libraries.

Libraries not included: The Moorland Spingarn Research Center.

The library director is an interim director. Professional positions include Associate Librarian, Librarian, Assistant/Associate Director, and Director. In addition, there are several special function positions held by persons with advanced degrees other than the MLS or MLIS.

## ILLINOIS, CHICAGO

Libraries included: Main campus library and Science Library.

Not included are the libraries of the Health Sciences in Chicago, Peoria, Rockford, Urbana.

There are eight levels in the University of Illinois, Chicago's rank system for professional librarians: 8 – Professor, 7 - Associate Professor, 6 - Assistant Professor, 5 - Clinical Professor, 4 - Clinical Associate Professor, 3 - Clinical Assistant Professor, 2 – Instructor, 1 - Academic Professional, 0 - University Librarian (not included in levels according to ARL instructions).

## ILLINOIS, URBANA

Libraries included: All main campus libraries.

## INDIANA

Libraries included: Main campus libraries.

Libraries not included: Dentistry Library; IUPUI University Library; Herron School of Art Library; Columbus Library; and Science and Engineering Library; and other campuses libraries at IU-East, IU-Kokomo, IU-Northwest, IU-Southeast, IU-South Bend, and IPFW-Fort Wayne.

**IOWA**

Libraries included: Main and six branches - one campus.

**IOWA STATE**

Libraries included: Parks Library (main library) and the Veterinary Medical Library (branch library).

**JOHNS HOPKINS**

Libraries included: Sheridan Libraries, Friedheim Library, SAIS Library.

**KANSAS**

Libraries included: The main campus Library and all branch libraries.

**KENT STATE**

Libraries included: Kent campus: main, architecture, chem/phys, fashion, map, performing arts; Kent State: Ashtabula, East Liverpool, Geauga, Salem, Stark, Trumbull, Tuscarawus.

**KENTUCKY**

Libraries included: William T Young Library (Main Campus Library); Agricultural Information Center; Design Library; Education Library; Engineering Library; Equine Library; Fine Arts Library; Science Library; Kentucky Transportation Center.

The Beginning Professional Salary (BPS) reported for the Law Library is for librarians with an MLS alone. The beginning salary for librarians with an MLS and JD is $52,000.

**LAVAL**

There is one library at Laval University (all included).

**LOUISVILLE**

Libraries included: Main, Art, Music, University Archives.

**MCGILL**

Libraries included: Humanities & Social Sciences, Islamic Studies, Education, Marvin Duchow Music, Schulich Library of Science and Engineering, Walter Hitschefeld Geographic Information Centre, Macdonald Campus, Howard Ross Library of Management.

McGill librarians ranks are: Tenure or non-tenured as Assistant Librarian, Associate Librarian, and Full Librarian.

**MCMASTER**

Libraries included: Mills Memorial Library, H.G. Thode Library, Innis Library.

**MANITOBA**

Libraries included: William R Newman Agriculture Library, Architecture and Fine Arts Library, Archives and Special Collections, Elizabeth Dafoe Library, Fr. Harold Drake Library, St. John's College Library, Donald W. Craik Engineering Library, Albert D. Cohen Management Library, Eckhardt-Gramattee Music Library, Sciences and Technology Library, Bill Larson Library, Carolyn Siftono-Helene Fuld Library, Concordia Hospital Library, J.W. Crane Memorial Library, Misercordia Health Centre Library, Riverview Health Centre Virtual Library, Seven Oaks General Hospital Library, Victoria General Hospital Library.

**MASSACHUSETTS**

Libraries included: DuBois Library, Science and Engineering Library, Image Collection Library.

## MIAMI

Libraries included: Main, Music, Architecture, Marine, Business.

## MICHIGAN

Libraries included: Area Programs; Art, Architecture, and Engineering; Asia; Askwith Media; Biological Station; Buhr Remote Shelving; Fine Arts; Foster; Government Documents; Hatcher Graduate; Map; Museums; Music; Papyrology; Shapiro Science; Shapiro Undergraduate; Special Collections.

Libraries not included: Bentley Historical; Clements; Gerald R. Ford Presidential; Kresge Business Administration; Law; Mardigian (Dearborn); Michigan Union; Thompson (Flint); University of Michigan Transportation; Research Institute; Weill Hall.

Figures are as of September 1, 2010. (Law Library)

Beginning salary with MLS only is $49,000. With MLS and JD it is $62,000. (Law Library)

## MICHIGAN STATE

Libraries included: Main and 5 branch libraries: Veterinary Medicine, Math, Engineering, Business & Gull Lake/Kellogg Biological Station.

## MISSOURI

Libraries included: Main, Engineering Library, Vet Medicine Library and University Archives.

## MIT

Libraries included: Barker Engineering Library, Science Library, Dewey Library for Management and Social Science, Rotch Library for Architecture and Planning, Humanities Library, Lewis Music Library, Institute Archives and Special Collections, library departments and administration.

There are eight levels in MIT's rank structure.

## MONTREAL

Libraries included: Environmental Development (www.bib.umontreal.ca/AM), Botany (www.bib.umontreal.ca/BV), Chemistry (www.bib.umontreal.ca/CH), Educational Resources (www.bib.umontreal.ca/DI), Education-Communication-Psychology-Psychoeducation-Biology (www.bib.umontreal.ca/ED), Geography (www.bib.umontreal.ca/GP), Kinesiology (www.bib.umontreal.ca/SA), Humanities and Social Sciences (www.bib.umontreal.ca/SS), Rare books and Special Collections (www.bib.umontreal.ca/GP), Mathematics and Computer Sciences (www.bib.umontreal.ca/MI), Veterinary (www.bib.umontreal.ca/SA), Music (www.bib.umontreal.ca/MU), Optometry (www.bib.umontreal.ca/SA), Physics (www.bib.umontreal.ca/PY), École polytechnique Library (www.polymtl.ca), HEC Montreal Library (www.hec.ca).

## NATIONAL LIBRARY OF MEDICINE

Data reported by the Federal fiscal year, which runs October 1 to September 30 of each calendar year.

## NEBRASKA

Libraries included: Geology Library, Math Library, Architecture Library, Music Library, Engineering Library.

## NEW MEXICO

Libraries included: Centennial Science & Engineering Library, Fine Arts & Design Library, Parish Memorial Library, Zimmerman Library.

Libraries not included: Gallup Branch Campus Library, Los Alamos Branch Campus Library, Taos Branch Campus, Library, Valencia Branch Campus Library.

Lecturers (Rank 1) salaries are higher than Assistant Professors (Rank 2) due to years of experience. (Law Library)

**NEW YORK**

Libraries included: Elmer Holmes Bobst Library, Institute of Fine Arts, Courant Institute of Mathematical Sciences Library, Institute for the Study of the Ancient World, Jack Brause Midtown Library.

Libraries not included: Bern Dibner Library at the Polytechnic Institute of NYU.

The three ranks are indicated as follows: 1. Library Associate, 2. Assistant Curator, 3. Associate Curator.

**NORTH CAROLINA STATE**

Libraries included: (Main) D.H. Hill Library, Design Library, Natural Resources Library, Textiles Library, Veterinary Medicine Library.

**NORTHWESTERN**

Libraries included: Main Library, Science & Engineering Library.

**NOTRE DAME**

Libraries included: The Hesburgh Libraries include - Hesburgh Library (Main), Architecture Library, Art Image Library, Business Information Center, Chemistry/Physics Library, Engineering Library, Kellogg/Kroc Information Center, and Mathematics Library.

**OHIO**

Libraries included: Main, Music, Depository, Learning Resource Center, Regional campuses (Eastern, Southern, Lancaster, Zanesville, Chillicothe).

The beginning salary applies to main campus hires only. The reference librarian salary that is below the listed beginning professional salary is employed on a branch campus.

**OHIO STATE**

Libraries included: Main and branch campus.

Main and Law salaries are as of 10/1/10; Health library salaries are as of 7/1/10.

**OKLAHOMA STATE**

Libraries included: OSU-Stillwater (Main, Vet Med, Architecture, Curriculum Materials); OSU-Oklahoma City; OSU-Okmulgee; OSU-Tulsa.

**OREGON**

Libraries included: Main (general) libraries include: Knight Library, Science Library, Architecture and Allied Arts Library, Portland Library and Learning Commons.

**OTTAWA**

Libraries included: Main campus Library (Morisset).

**PENNSYLVANIA**

Libraries included: University library, Lippincott (business), math/physics (physical sciences), fine arts, veterinary, museum, Center for Advanced Judaic Studies, rare book and manuscript, music.

Libraries not included: Annenberg (communications).

## PENNSYLVANIA STATE

Libraries included: University Park (main campus), Abington, Altoona, Beaver, Berks, Brandywine, DuBois, Erie, Fayette, Great Valley, Greater Allegheny, Harrisburg, Hazleton, Lehigh Valley, Mont Alto, New Kensington, Shenango, Schuylkill, Wilkes-Barre, Worthington-Scranton, and York..

## PITTSBURGH

Libraries included: University Library System and library directors at regional libraries - Titusville, Johnstown, Bradford, and Greensburg.

Libraries not included: All other staff at regional libraries - Titusville, Johnstown, Bradford, and Greensburg.

## PRINCETON

Libraries included: Firestone Library, East Asian Library, Marquand Library of Art and Archaeology, Lewis Library (Science and Technology Libraries), Engineering Library, Psychology, Mudd Manuscript Library, Cotsen Children's Library, Mendel Music Library, School of Architecture Library and Stokes Library.

## PURDUE

Libraries included: The library system on the West Lafayette campus, consisting of 11 subject-oriented libraries, an undergraduate library, and a special collections research center.

Libraries not included: Libraries at the regional campuses; Purdue North Central (Westville), Purdue Calumet (Hammond) and Indiana University-Purdue University, Fort Wayne.

The four-level rank structure for Purdue Libraries data uses ranks 2 through 4 for Libraries faculty positions: Rank 2 for Assistant Professors, Rank 3 for Associate Professors, and Rank 4 for (Full) Professors. Rank 1 is used for other professional positions; this is a broad category of non-faculty professional positions. These positions include positions that require an MLIS or other advanced degree but are not faculty positions, IT professionals, director of advancement, and other professional staff. Due to market differentials in salaries among various professions and differences in longevity of incumbents, some salaries in Rank 1 are higher than some salaries of Ranks 2 through 4.

## QUEEN'S

Libraries included: Stauffer (Humanities & Social Science), Douglas (Engineering/Science), Jordan (Special Collections/Music), Education.

## ROCHESTER

Libraries included: River Campus Libraries & Sibley Music Library.

## RUTGERS

Libraries included: Research and Instructional Services, John Cotton Dana Library and Branches, Paul Robeson Library, Technical and Automated Services.

Libraries not included: Alexander Library, Mabel Smith Douglass Library, Kilmer Library, Library of Science and Medicine and Branches, School of Management and Labor Relations, Center for Alcohol Studies.

## SASKATCHEWAN

Libraries included: Murray Library, Education & Music Library, Natural Sciences Library, Veterinary Medicine Library, and Engineering Library.

## SOUTH CAROLINA

Libraries included: Thomas Cooper (main) Library, Business Library, Math Library, Music Library, South Caroliniana Library, Moving Image Research Collections.

## SOUTHERN CALIFORNIA

Libraries included: Main campus libraries.


## SUNY-ALBANY

Libraries included: Main campus and branch libraries.


## SUNY-BUFFALO

Libraries included: The Arts & Sciences Libraries, Music Library, and Special Collections (University Archives, The Poetry Collection and Rare & Special Books).

Salary information for classified staff, employees at the SL-2 salary level and temporary hires was not included.


## SUNY-STONY BROOK

Libraries included: Main campus.


## SYRACUSE

Libraries included: Main campus library, Science & Technology library, Geology & Math libraries.

Libraries not included: College reading rooms.


## TEMPLE

Libraries included: Paley Library; Science & Engineering Library; Ambler Campus Library.

Salary for Director for Library Advancement & External Relations is reported in full, but is split between Libraries and University Advancement (Development) Office.

Minimum beginning professional salary of $44,004.00 is based on an 11-month contract. Minimum beginning salary for a 10-month contract is $40,150.


## TENNESSEE

Libraries included: Main (University of Tennessee) Library.

Health includes the Memphis Health Sciences Library and Knoxville Hospital Medical Library.


## TEXAS

Figures are as of August 31, 2010.

Libraries included: Dolph Briscoe Center for American History, Harry Ransom Humanities Research Center, and the University of Texas Libraries.


## TEXAS A&M

Libraries included: Sterling C. Evans Library, Library Annex, Cushing Memorial Library, Medical Sciences Library, Policy Sciences & Economics Library, West Campus Library.

Libraries not included: Texas A&M University Library at Qatar, Jack K. Williams Library (Galveston, TX), Technical Resource Center (Architecture Library).

**TEXAS TECH**

Figures are as of September 1, 2010.

Libraries included: University Library, Southwest Collections/Special Collections Library, Vietnam Archives.

**VANDERBILT**

Libraries included: The Central Library, Divinity Library, Peabody Library, Management Library, Music Library, Science and Engineering Library, Special Collections and University Archives, centralized Technical Services, Library Administration and Television News Archive.

**VIRGINIA**

Libraries included: University of Virginia Library, Darden Graduate Business Library, Excludes the John Cook Wyllie Library at the University of Virginia College at Wise.

Libraries not included: University of Virginia College at Wise.

**VIRGINIA TECH**

Libraries included: Vet Med Library, Art and Architecture Library.

**WASHINGTON**

Libraries included: Libraries on the Seattle, Bothell and Tacoma campuses of the University of Washington.

**WASHINGTON STATE**

Libraries included: WSU Pullman, main campus, WSU Spokane, WSU Tri-Cities, WSU Vancouver, WSU Energy Library.

**WASHINGTON UNIVERSITY IN ST. LOUIS**

Libraries included: Art & Architecture, Business, Chemistry, Earth & Planetary Sciences, East Asian, Music, Physics, Social Work, West Campus.

**WATERLOO**

Libraries included: The Dana Porter; Davis Centre; University Map Library and Musagetes Architecture Libraries.

We have a 6-level rank structure.

**WAYNE STATE**

Libraries included: The Purdy/Kresge Library, Science and Engineering Library, and Undergraduate Library.

Libraries not included: The Reuther Archives of Labor and Urban Affairs.

**WESTERN ONTARIO**

Libraries included: The D.B. Weldon Library, Business Library, Education Library, Music Library, Allyn & Betty Taylor Library.

Libraries not included: Affiliated College Libraries - King's University College Library, Huron University College Library and Brescia University College Library.

**WISCONSIN**

Libraries included: Memorial, Archives, College, Steenbock Agricultural and Life Science, Art, Biology, Business, Chemistry, Geography, Geology, Math, Music, Physics, Social Work, Special collections, Social Science Reading Room, Wendt Engineering.

Libraries not included: Wisconsin Historical Society, Center for Instructional Media, SLIS, Robinson Map Library, Primate Center.

**YALE**

Libraries included: Arts Library (Robert B. Haas Family Arts Library), Bass Library (Anne T. & Robert M. Bass Library), Beinecke Rare Book and Manuscript Library, Chemistry Library (Sterling Chemistry Library), Classics Library, Divinity School Library, East Asia Library, Engineering and Applied Science Library, Forestry and Environmental Studies Library, Geology Library, Government Documents and Information Center, Lewis Walpole Library, Mathematics Library, Mudd Library, Music Library (Irving S. Gilmore Music Library), Science Library (Kline Science Library), Social Science Library, Sterling Memorial Library.

**YORK**

Libraries included: York University Libraries.

# ARL Member Libraries as of January 1, 2011

The Association of Research Libraries (ARL) represents the interests of 126 libraries that serve major North American research institutions. ARL operates as a forum for the exchange of ideas and as an agent for collective action to influence the forces affecting the ability of these libraries to meet the future needs of scholarship. The ARL Statistics and Measurement program is organized around identifying, collecting, analyzing, and distributing quantifiable information describing the characteristics of research libraries. The program offers publications and special member services, and collaborates with other national and international library statistics programs.

| Institution | Category | Full Name of Institution | Location |
|---|---|---|---|
| Alabama | S | University of Alabama | Tuscaloosa, Alabama |
| Alberta | C | University of Alberta | Edmonton, Alberta |
| Arizona | S | University of Arizona | Tucson, Arizona |
| Arizona State | S | Arizona State University | Tempe, Arizona |
| Auburn | S | Auburn University | Auburn, Alabama |
| Boston | P | Boston University | Boston, Massachusetts |
| Boston College | P | Boston College | Boston, Massachusetts |
| Brigham Young | P | Brigham Young University | Provo, Utah |
| British Columbia | C | University of British Columbia | Vancouver, British Columbia |
| Brown | P | Brown University | Providence, Rhode Island |
| Berkeley, California | S | University of California, Berkeley | California, Berkeley |
| Calgary | C | University of Calgary | Calgary, Alberta |
| California, Davis | S | University of California, Davis | Davis, California |
| California, Irvine | S | University of California, Irvine | Irvine, California |
| California, Los Angeles | S | University of California, Los Angeles | Los Angeles, California |
| California, Riverside | S | University of California, Riverside | Riverside, California |
| California, San Diego | S | University of California, San Diego | La Jolla, California |
| California, Santa Barbara | S | University of California, Santa Barbara | Santa Barbara, California |
| Case Western Reserve | P | Case Western Reserve University | Cleveland, Ohio |
| Chicago | P | University of Chicago | Chicago, Illinois |
| Cincinnati | S | University of Cincinnati | Cincinnati, Ohio |
| Colorado | S | University of Colorado | Boulder, Colorado |
| Colorado State | S | Colorado State University | Fort Collins, Colorado |
| Columbia | P | Columbia University | New York, New York |
| Connecticut | S | University of Connecticut | Storrs, Connecticut |
| Cornell | P | Cornell University | Ithaca, New York |
| Dartmouth | P | Dartmouth College | Hanover, New Hampshire |
| Delaware | S | University of Delaware | Newark, Delaware |
| Duke | P | Duke University | Durham, North Carolina |
| Emory | P | Emory University | Atlanta, Georgia |
| Florida | S | University of Florida | Gainesville, Florida |
| Florida State | S | Florida State University | Tallahassee, Florida |
| George Washington | P | George Washington University | Washington, DC |
| Georgetown | P | Georgetown University | Washington, DC |

| Institution | Category | Full Name of Institution | Location |
| --- | --- | --- | --- |
| Georgia | S | University of Georgia | Athens, Georgia |
| Georgia Tech | S | Georgia Institute of Technology | Atlanta, Georgia |
| Guelph | C | University of Guelph | Guelph, Ontario |
| Harvard | P | Harvard University | Cambridge, Massachusetts |
| Hawaii | S | University of Hawaii | Honolulu, Hawaii |
| Houston | S | University of Houston | Houston, Texas |
| Howard | P | Howard University | Washington, DC |
| Illinois, Chicago | S | University of Illinois at Chicago | Chicago, Illinois |
| Illinois, Urbana | S | University of Illinois at Urbana | Urbana, Illinois |
| Indiana | S | Indiana University | Bloomington, Indiana |
| Iowa | S | University of Iowa | Iowa City, Iowa |
| Iowa State | S | Iowa State University | Ames, Iowa |
| Johns Hopkins | P | Johns Hopkins University | Baltimore, Maryland |
| Kansas | S | University of Kansas | Lawrence, Kansas |
| Kent State | S | Kent State University | Kent, Ohio |
| Kentucky | S | University of Kentucky | Lexington, Kentucky |
| Laval | C | Laval University | Quebec, Quebec |
| Louisiana State | S | Louisiana State University | Baton Rouge, Louisiana |
| Louisville | S | University of Louisville | Louisville, Kentucky |
| McGill | C | McGill University | Montreal, Quebec |
| McMaster | C | McMaster University | Hamilton, Ontario |
| Manitoba | C | University of Manitoba | Winnipeg, Manitoba |
| Maryland | S | University of Maryland | College Park, Maryland |
| Massachusetts | S | University of Massachusetts | Amherst, Massachusetts |
| MIT | P | Massachusetts Institute of Technology | Cambridge, Massachusetts |
| Miami | P | University of Miami | Coral Gables, Florida |
| Michigan | S | University of Michigan | Ann Arbor, Michigan |
| Michigan State | S | Michigan State University | East Lansing, Michigan |
| Minnesota | S | University of Minnesota | Minneapolis, Minnesota |
| Missouri | S | University of Missouri | Columbia, Missouri |
| Montreal | C | University of Montreal | Montreal, Quebec |
| Nebraska | S | University of Nebraska-Lincoln | Lincoln, Nebraska |
| New Mexico | S | University of New Mexico | Albuquerque, New Mexico |
| New York | P | New York University | New York, New York |
| North Carolina | S | University of North Carolina | Chapel Hill, North Carolina |
| North Carolina State | S | North Carolina State University | Raleigh, North Carolina |
| Northwestern | P | Northwestern University | Evanston, Illinois |
| Notre Dame | P | University of Notre Dame | Notre Dame, Indiana |
| Ohio | S | Ohio University | Athens, Ohio |
| Ohio State | S | Ohio State University | Columbus, Ohio |
| Oklahoma | S | University of Oklahoma | Norman, Oklahoma |
| Oklahoma State | S | Oklahoma State University | Stillwater, Oklahoma |

| Institution | Category | Full Name of Institution | Location |
| --- | --- | --- | --- |
| Oregon | S | University of Oregon | Eugene, Oregon |
| Ottawa | C | University of Ottawa | Ottawa, Ontario |
| Pennsylvania | P | University of Pennsylvania | Philadelphia, Pennsylvania |
| Pennsylvania State | S | Pennsylvania State University | University Park, Pennsylvania |
| Pittsburgh | S | University of Pittsburgh | Pittsburgh, Pennsylvania |
| Princeton | P | Princeton University | Princeton, New Jersey |
| Purdue | S | Purdue University | West Lafayette, Indiana |
| Queen's | C | Queen's University | Kingston, Ontario |
| Rice | P | Rice University | Houston, Texas |
| Rochester | P | University of Rochester | Rochester, New York |
| Rutgers | S | Rutgers University | New Brunswick, New Jersey |
| Saskatchewan | C | University of Saskatchewan | Saskatoon, Saskatchewan |
| South Carolina | S | University of South Carolina | Columbia, South Carolina |
| Southern California | P | University of Southern California | Los Angeles, California |
| Southern Illinois | S | Southern Illinois University | Carbondale, Illinois |
| SUNY-Albany | S | University at Albany, State University of New York | Albany, New York |
| SUNY-Buffalo | S | University at Buffalo, State University of New York | Buffalo, New York |
| SUNY-Stony Brook | S | State University of New York at Stony Brook | Stony Brook, New York |
| Syracuse | P | Syracuse University | Syracuse, New York |
| Temple | S | Temple University | Philadelphia, Pennsylvania |
| Tennessee | S | University of Tennessee | Knoxville, Tennessee |
| Texas | S | University of Texas | Austin, Texas |
| Texas A&M | S | Texas A&M University | College Station, Texas |
| Texas Tech | S | Texas Tech University | Lubbock, Texas |
| Toronto | C | University of Toronto | Toronto, Ontario |
| Tulane | P | Tulane University | New Orleans, Louisiana |
| Utah | S | University of Utah | Salt Lake City, Utah |
| Vanderbilt | P | Vanderbilt University | Nashville, Tennessee |
| Virginia | S | University of Virginia | Charlottesville, Virginia |
| Virginia Tech | S | Virginia Polytechnic Institute & State University | Blacksburg, Virginia |
| Washington | S | University of Washington | Seattle, Washington |
| Washington State | S | Washington State University | Pullman, Washington |
| Washington U.-St. Louis | P | Washington University | St. Louis, Missouri |
| Waterloo | C | University of Waterloo | Waterloo, Ontario |
| Wayne State | S | Wayne State University | Detroit, Michigan |
| Western Ontario | C | University of Western Ontario | London, Ontario |
| Wisconsin | S | University of Wisconsin | Madison, Wisconsin |
| Yale | P | Yale University | New Haven, Connecticut |
| York | C | York University | North York, Ontario |
|  |  |  |  |
| Boston Public Library | N | Boston Public Library | Boston, Massachusetts |
| Canada Inst. SciTech Info. | X | Canada Inst. for Scientific & Technical Information | Ottawa, Ontario |

| Institution | Category | Full Name of Institution | Location |
| --- | --- | --- | --- |
| Center for Research Libs. | N | Center for Research Libraries | Chicago, Illinois |
| Lib. & Archives Canada | X | Library and Archives Canada | Ottawa, Ontario |
| Library of Congress | N | Library of Congress | Washington, DC |
| Natl. Agricultural Lib. | N | National Agricultural Library | Beltsville, Maryland |
| Natl. Archives & Records | N | National Archives and Records Administration | Washington, DC |
| Natl. Library of Medicine | N | National Library of Medicine | Bethesda, Maryland |
| New York Public Library | N | New York Public Library | New York, New York |
| New York State Library | N | New York State Library | Albany, New York |
| Smithsonian Institution | N | Smithsonian Institution | Washington, DC |

S – US public university
P – US private university
C – Canadian university
N – US nonuniversity
X – Canadian nonuniversity

Made in the USA
Charleston, SC
17 December 2011